Hate or Be Hated
How I Survived Right-Wing Extremism

JG Daniel

ISBN: 978-1-48357-096-9 (print)
ISBN-978-1-48357-097-9 (ebook)

DEDICATION

For my wife & son

CONTENTS

ACKNOWLEDGMENTS

It's with all of my love that I thank my wife for standing by me throughout the writing of this book and the rants that came about from this process. She rarely saw any of the content during the five years or so it took me to complete this. She was incredibly patient and very supportive and without her by my side urging me to be the best father and husband I could be, there's no doubt in my mind that I'd still be a miserable person in denial.

To my son, you rock my world. You are my greatest achievement and my greatest joy. You're the coolest person I've ever known. I am so proud that I'm your dad. Be yourself - always!

To Mom and Dad, this book isn't for you even though I'm sure you think it is. The writing of this book ultimately opened my eyes to what has been real throughout my life and what has not.

To my three siblings, I wish we were closer. Perhaps there will be a day when there will be no animosity or judgement and we can all just get along and enjoy each other's families. I sincerely hope so.

I am incredibly grateful for the help, direction and loving advice from Nancy who believed in me and this book. Because of all your tough questions, I ended rewriting most of this book. Your dedication was unwavering and thank you again for protecting me from who I used to be.

Patricia, your advice and enthusiastic support for this project has been so appreciated. Your professionalism in helping me understand what I wanted to say has been invaluable. Your reasoning and energy helped me get to the finish line.

Special thanks to Dr. Jeff for your encouragement and advice. I always enjoy talking with you and without your advice early on, this book wouldn't exist.

Thank you Rob for being there to let me know I wasn't crazy. Thank you to Joel, my brother from another mother, who has shown me that family isn't necessarily about blood. Thank you to Roger for showing me what a real friend looks like. And thank you to Karen for being there and being someone I can be proud of.

I need to thank the grown man in my life who stepped up at times to be a father figure for me. I know you don't believe it, but you saved my life back in high school Chuck. I can't thank you enough for everything you've done for me.

Claire Connor, thank you for writing your book, *Wrapped in the Flag*. After I read it, I knew I wasn't alone in being raised by right-wing extremists and I knew I had to tell my story too.

KILL 'EM ALL

I was twelve years-old, lying face down on my belly in the prone position in front of our old doublewide trailer which was situated in the woods of Western Washington. The nearest neighbor was nearly a half mile away. As usual it was wet outside and the ground was cold and soggy. The muddy driveway had a bend in it about fifty yards away, where at any moment the enemy could be coming right at me. In my hands was one of Dad's converted, full auto AR-15's and it was loaded.

The excited warning coming out of his mouth was, "Russian jeeps coming up the driveway!" This meant pull the trigger. I held my breath. I was poised on edge, my finger on the trigger, ready to fire. "Kill 'em all! Kill 'em all!" he yelled. Dad asked if I killed 'em all. I said "I did. I killed them all." The thirty round bullet clip was empty. Dad was happy. And so was I.

I was thirteen when I wrote my first "Letter to the Editor" to the local newspaper. It was my patriotic duty to correct the editorial board of *The News Tribune* regarding what form of government we had in the United States. Often the newspaper used the word "democracy" to describe America's form of government and not only was this wrong, it was misleading. Democracies lead to dictatorships I was taught, and we were being duped by the media on a daily basis.

The United States was a "constitutional republic" - a government based on the principals of laws and it was my absolute duty to inform them of this. My letter was published.

The Editorial Board and all of their readers now knew the truth. Dad was happy. And so was I.

I took a copy of my published letter to school and showed it to my friends. You can imagine how awesome my classmates must have thought I was. I glowingly showed it to some of my teachers as well. Yes, I was that kid.

A year later I decided that I wanted to be a mercenary after I graduated so I could kill commies and dictators to ensure that America would never perish. I revealed this in my high school Careers class. My report discussed the pros and cons of killing people for a living. The only struggle I had with writing the report had to do with whether or not I could kill anyone. I concluded I could if the price was right. Killing a liberal would be easy. I got a C- on my report. Dad was happy. And so was I.

It was only a couple of years later when I received my formal "training" during the summer of 1985 at a John Birch Society summer camp located at the YMCA Campgrounds in Lake Wenatchee, WA., about three hours east of Seattle. I would be one among hundreds of teenagers sent to your not-so-average summer camp to learn the secrets of the Grand Communist Conspiracy. I would also learn how my own high school teachers were trying to brainwash me into becoming a liberal like them and then eventually a full-on commie.

The John Birch Society summer camp featured daily lectures about how rock and roll was going to make me love Satan and how the United Nations was created to take away our freedoms and ultimately destroy America with their New World Order, among other topics. I was taught that democrats, liberals, bankers, the government, celebrities and the media were all working together to trick us into becoming communist slaves. Most importantly, however, I was taught that the John Birch Society was the only organization which could ultimately save America from the communist threat and preserve our freedoms. I learned they were our only hope to make America great again. I didn't believe everything I was taught, but a lot of it I did.

In a nutshell, the John Birch Society is by far the most radical anti-communist and anti-government organization on the planet. It was created by a few wealthy Americans who wish to preserve their wealth and their interpretation of the American Dream by putting the fear of totalitarian slavery and misery into the hearts and minds of gullible and illogical American fools.

While other kids were having fun in the early eighties, I was stressing out that America was going to be overrun by communists. Educating friends and others with the truth was awkward. To keep my mouth shut meant that I was "sitting on the fence," as Dad would say, and that meant I was assisting the Conspiracy in its quest. Most American teenagers aren't that concerned about the end of the world so my warnings often fell on deaf ears. Many times I wouldn't say anything just to try to fit in and be somewhat normal, though when I did this I always felt like I was letting Dad down.

During these years of my upbringing we were prepping before they called it "prepping." We were readying for a fight - an invasion from enemy troops, martial law, nuclear or chemical war or some other disastrous threat. It didn't matter what the fight was or how or where it was coming from – we knew that the shit was going to hit the fan real soon and we'd rather fight and die than become communists.

Dad always said we'd be lucky to survive another year before something would destroy America. He's been saying this every year for as long I can remember and of course still does to this day. For most of my early teenage years, due to the brainwashing and my naivety, I struggled against allowing myself to have any reasonable thoughts as I shared Dad's sentiments.

Dad was the smartest person I'd ever known up to this point in my life, and he said the truth was always hidden, twisted or covered up by liberals, communists, the government or the media. No matter what obvious and reasonable facts were presented in any given situation, Dad always sided with the extreme right-wing conservative stance - even if it wasn't true. The truth was irrelevant. Whatever he was told by the John Birch Society, the National Rifle Association or any other extreme right-wing organization was the absolute truth in his mind. He'd read their propaganda like a preacher reads his bible and nothing could ever be questioned.

If the John Birch Society said there were five hundred million Chinese soldiers hiding near the US/Mexico border getting ready to invade us, he'd believe it and would be warning you about it, without any proof or evidence. If you didn't believe him, he'd think you were an idiot. His mind has been lost for decades to the propaganda of the extreme right which seeks nothing more than to scare the shit out of all of us by using conspiracy theories and deceptive ideas.

Dad's a confused Vietnam Vet who hated the war and our government for sending him over there. He's only alive because he came back to say goodbye to his dying father. While he was home his platoon back in Vietnam got wiped out. The Army didn't send him back to Vietnam. It's a horrible story that I can't even begin to imagine. As war protests increased at home with the long hairs and intellectuals taking the lead, and with Dad's unfounded hatred for hippies, smart people and anyone who didn't share his thoughts, he began to defend the war. His failure to comprehend that these people were protesting the senseless deaths of his buddies is yet another manifestation of his hatred-driven actions.

Dad's had a serious case of survivor's guilt since the war, which has shaped his miserable existence. Many times when I was a kid, he'd tell me that he wished he was dead or wished he'd never married my mom. I always felt bad when he'd say that. I used to believe that I was the reason he was so lost and felt his life was wasted. This was in the eighties. He's still alive today, still miserable and still wasting away.

I've tried so hard to make him happy that it consumes me. I've overachieved with most of the things that I've attempted in order to let him know that he was in some way successful with me. Making Dad proud of me has been the main motivator in my existence. My complete feeling of being a failure to him, however, came with the realization that there's nothing I can do to make him proud of me. Anything I do that doesn't replicate his own miserable existence is a waste of time in his eyes. By not being him, I've failed him.

He has accomplished little, if anything at all, in dealing with his survivor's guilt from that stupid war. That, combined with his deep hatred for our government and his own personal shame, made him a horrific father and person. He was a scary, psychopathic husband with a wife who feared him and was careful not to do anything to upset him.

His distorted view of the world, much less America, is based upon his closed-minded fundamental belief that "they" are out to get us. "They" is everything and anything that has to do with destroying America: blacks, Jews, gays, communists, socialists, Marxists, humanists, liberals, democrats, environmentalists, educators, equal rights proponents, foreigners, people of color, rich people, happy people or anyone else who contradicted him. His anger made him a natural fit with the racist, right-wing conspiracy-minded militant nut jobs who believed Joseph McCarthy to be an honorable American while John F. Kennedy and Martin Luther King Jr. were commies set out to destroy America.

Dad is a poor man who hates welfare and government, yet would be homeless without his disability pension, Social Security check, VA benefits and the under-the-table cash he receives for leasing out his property. Those who truly know him and aren't like him see him as a self-righteous, racially bigoted man who lies, cheats and steals and is the biggest hypocrite they've ever known. He's a miserable person and has been since the day I was born.

My dad hates me. He trained me to be just like him. He hates me because I'm not like him. He hates me because I'm open-minded and compassionate. He hates me because I don't hate others. He hates me because by failing to program me he has assisted the Communist Conspiracy in its quest to overthrow America.

I'm not my dad. I'm an American and a veteran and not totally proud of either.

Mom says to me, "your father loves you, but just doesn't know how to show it." She's been saying this for decades. She only says this because deep inside she knows that he's never loved anyone including her, except perhaps his mother and Claymore, his dead Rottweiler. Mother is in complete denial that she wasted over forty years with a man who never loved her. By claiming "he just doesn't know how to show it," even years after divorcing him, she is still lying for him, to herself and me.

Since I was seventeen, I've worked hard to not be anything like my dad. I've countered much of the ideology and negativity that was ingrained in me, but it's been a struggle overcoming the lack of reasonable and honest judgment that was omitted from my upbringing.

Had I stayed the course, been loyal to his ideals, there's no question in my mind that I'd likely be dead or would have demonstrated a similar moronic and catastrophic terror like that of Timothy McVeigh, the "good son," for example. If I hadn't wrenched myself out of the deep end, I imagine I would've had some significant role with the Tea Party and the current wave of right-wing extremism eroding and trying to take over this country. These are the only scenarios in my mind where I can think my father would actually be proud of me.

This is my story. Or maybe it's my dad's story. Ultimately, it's a story about my anger and embarrassment over who I was and how I was raised in an environment that didn't value empathy, honesty and caring. I am angry and embarrassed that I still struggle with the impact of my upbringing. I am angry and embarrassed that on some level, I still want my dad to be proud of me.

Some might call the brainwashing I experienced a form of child abuse. For decades I thought I had a somewhat normal childhood. No child should experience the paranoia, despair and isolation that Dad instilled in me. No child should be taught by radical right-wing American extremists that the only options in this life are to "hate or be hated."

INTRODUCTION

Since the end of World War II, millions of gullible white Americans have been inundated with the fear that communism is spreading throughout the world and more importantly in the United States.

America's wealthy extreme right has a vested interest in maintaining and feeding this fear so they can expand their great wealth and preserve an economic system that benefits them alone. The Koch Brothers, their father before them and others have created a web of distortions filled with lies and conspiracy theories. Their intention is to captivate and enslave the minds of millions of regular Americans so they will believe everything they are fed from some right-wing media entities.

These include certain programming on Fox News, people like Glen Beck and Rush Limbaugh, as well as organizations like The John Birch Society, Americans for Prosperity, the Tea Party and others.

When American parents force feed, indoctrinate and brainwash their children into their culture of right-wing extremism and American fanaticism, the effect on them can be overwhelming.

Childhood and puberty are tough enough as it is. It is a horrible and despicable act to instill fear, hate, despair, isolationism, paranoia, entitlement and a romantic obsession for domestic terrorism in a young mind.

My father brought me into this world to help save the country from communist enslavement. His intended purpose for my life was to educate others with the truth about the Communist Conspiracy and to help set America free.

This book is about my personal journey and the way these attitudes directly caused so much suffering in my own life as well as how it is still having an effect on the choices and decisions being made by a large percentage of people in this country today.

1 FORTUNATE SON

In 1945, the United States detonated an atomic bomb on Hiroshima, the United Nations was formed and my dad was born. I know more about the atomic bomb and the U.N. than I do about my dad's childhood. This is true despite the fact he raised me and my siblings, with all of us living together, until I moved out at age seventeen.

Dad grew up in a small town in Western Washington. On the biggest day of the year in October, they'd have a parade which signified the opening day of deer hunting season. I grew up in that same town.

I was born at Fort Lewis, WA in 1968. Mom, Dad and I moved to California after I was born and lived there until we moved back to Washington in 1974.

During that time in California, we lived in a sketchy neighborhood in Pacoima, a small town in the San Fernando Valley that was home to a lot of Mexicans. Looking back, we were rather poor and barely average for that community. I went to a predominately Mexican Catholic school. I remember having a red wagon and collecting Coors aluminum cans in it. Mom used to tell me that all my friends (I was four at the time) were Mexicans. I remember Dad hated that. He said Mexicans were taking over California.

Dad was depressed living in California. Too many "wetbacks," he'd say, and I'm sure all the other non-white people made him angry too. In the small town he was from in Western Washington it was all white expect for one Hawaiian/Japanese farming family.

Dad never talked about his school experiences much. He says he graduated in 1963, but he never did receive a high school diploma. These days, however, he's involved with the alumni from his high school. He never went to college and I'm not really sure what he did after high school other than an odd job here and there and then his time in the military.

Four years after leaving high school, Dad was drafted and went into the army. It was 1967 and the United States was at war with Vietnam. He was a grunt or a foot soldier in the war with no specialty other than pulling the trigger on his gun.

To this day, he's never talked to me about the war or what happened to him over there other than getting really angry concerning the topic of soldiers left behind or "Missing in Action," or about things we saw in war movies together. I think I was afraid to ask about his experiences in Vietnam when I was younger. Mom said not to bring it up as talking about the war would upset him, so I never did.

The only real story I do know about Dad and his experience with the war is not a pretty one. It's quite sad, and it was told to me by Mom. After a short time of being over there in the war, my dad's father (my grandpa) was dying and in the hospital back in Tacoma, WA. It was October 1967. Apparently when you have a direct family member about to die and you're out fighting in a war, the military grants you emergency leave. Because of this, they flew Dad back home to Washington State to be with his dying father.

While he was back home, his dad died. My dad was very upset of course, but even worse, days later while he was waiting to fly back to Vietnam to reengage with his buddies, he gets word that his entire platoon, including his best friend, were all killed while out on a mission. Each and every soldier in dad's platoon was dead. Everyone he knew in the Vietnam War had been killed.

Had he not come home, he'd surely be dead too.

Sad as all this is, it's a good thing for my existence that Dad did come home, because otherwise I wouldn't be here today.

He was kept stateside and within a year, I was born.

I'm certain he was incredibly depressed and didn't deal with his survivor's guilt from the tragedy involving his former platoon in Vietnam. Who wouldn't be overwhelmed with this? Where was the Army in providing him with the necessary therapy to help him cope and heal from such a tragedy? Dad went through some heavy stuff and I can't even imagine that he is able to get through a single day without thinking about it. I feel terrible for him.

Dad doesn't like many people and doesn't have many friends. Unfortunately, I'm kind of the same way.

He always had and has an opinion about everyone and everything. "He's a decent guy except for that long hair," he'd say. "For a Mexican, he sure is a hard worker. "Your uncle's a good guy, except he's got too much of that Jewish blood in him." Those who didn't agree with his thoughts were stupid in his eyes. Those who didn't care about the things he did were worthless to him. Dad was an angry person. He looked for other angry people to justify his own anger. He always had to have an enemy. He still does to this day.

In our house, Dad would get angry at the TV with liberal shows like *M.A.S.H.* (goofy liberal war show), the *Mary Tyler Moore Show* (an independent career woman) and others. I remember him walking up to the TV and turning it off saying, "I'm sick of watching this leftwing crap and I won't have my children being brainwashed by it!" He would glare at my Mom when he'd yell this. Of course, he'd walk out of the room and Mom would look at us and tell us to go play in our bedrooms. *Little House on the Prairie* and *Hee Haw* were two shows we could watch without Dad getting angry

Dad was angry because Hollywood was promoting "un-American" themes on television. *Mary Tyler Moore* was unacceptable because she was a non-married woman pursuing a career, which was against the concept of the fundamental American family with a dad working, a mom birthing and cleaning house.

This programming upset a lot of Americans. I was taught it was numbing us and setting us on a path to welcome in communism. I always thought his behavior was ridiculous and embarrassing, but nonetheless, his impact has been lasting.

Dad found comfort for his narrow views of what was wrong and what was right with America and other Americans. He found it in an organization that was very strong in the middle-class white neighborhoods of Southern California. This was, after all, an area under siege in the late sixties and early seventies with lots of racial and immigration issues. It was during this time when affirmative action and women's lib were making gains. Dad wasn't alone with his anger. Mom saw this and supported her husband.

Dad's views were similar to those of some other people and were justified in his mind and likely mother's - only because they all felt the same way. When people act on strong feelings, they tend to gravitate to other people with similar feelings. They can easily become convinced of a false certainty that their beliefs are "fact." These people that Dad gravitated to believed they knew what was wrong with America and they believed they needed to save our country from the greatest threat of all - communism. This was when Dad was introduced to the John Birch Society and found other weak-minded, hate-filled Americans just like himself.

2. THE JOHN BIRCH SOCIETY

"For the truth I bring you is simple, incontrovertible and deadly. It is that, unless we can reverse forces which now seem inexorable in their movement, you have only a few more years before the country in which you live will become four separate provinces in a world-wide communist dominion ruled by police-state methods from the Kremlin..." - 1958, Robert Welch, founder of the John Birch Society.[1]

For over half a century now, the John Birch Society has been the most radical anti-communist and anti-government organization in the history of the United States. It was created by a few wealthy and angry Americans who feared losing their wealth and their interpretation of the American Dream. Their strategy was and is to inject the fear of totalitarian slavery into the hearts and minds of millions of gullible and illogical, unhappy Americans.

The founders of the Birch Society believe a group of men called the Illuminati are the forefathers of communism and that they work hand in hand with Satan in a conspiracy to eliminate America.[2]

Birchers warn that we have little time left and if we don't act soon to save America, all will be lost. They've been saying this with great panic and fear for over half a century now. The Society boasts that the only weapon in fighting this conspiracy is with their "truth."

The leadership in the John Birch Society does this with constant brainwashing of their followers. They do this with scare tactics and a conspiracy philosophy that preaches to anyone who will listen to them that America will surely perish if you don't join them in the fight now. They want you to invest in them with your money and time. They'll "educate" you on whom to vote for and they'll tell you to get your friends and family to do the same.

The Society is very much like a cult, except that it boasts a private and secret membership with a wide variety of religious affiliations. They're an organization with chapters set up in each and every state. At one point, they had over 400 of their American Opinion Bookstores operating in America. They have monthly meetings in living rooms all over the country. They have "action items" (letter writing campaigns, call your congressman scripts, put up signage, as well as other activities) that are necessary for members to complete each month. They encourage members to host speaking events and community meetings in their homes. They set up booths at local fairs to recruit new members. They buy billboards all over our highway systems. Occasionally, they buy advertising in newspapers to sway public opinion. They encourage home-schooling and provide their own curriculum so children can avoid the indoctrination of communism in the public schools.

My early teenage years were mostly guided by Dad's leadership and the example he set. Dad was like an obedient zombie when it came to the propaganda from the John Birch Society. Anything put out by the Society in their *American Opinion* newsletter or *The New American* magazine was considered gospel. Their books, videos and instructions were held up to be "the truth." Being the good obedient son that I was, I clung to each and every word and message as if it were an absolute truth.

Dad was literal in this as his support and dedication to the John Birch Society was his top priority in life. It was his pulse, his directive and his purpose. Dad's dedication to the Birch Society was higher than his dedication to his family, his wife, his children, his friends, and his god and ultimately even higher than his dedication to America. Dad was down in the dumps so when he discovered the John Birch Society and joined, it gave him purpose.

Most people like my father get suckered in to the John Birch Society because they suffer from low self-esteem, paranoia and fear of the unknown. These people are then fed inflammatory information to ignite their frustration and anger, after which all they do is think, say and preach irresponsible and hateful things.

The John Birch Society was formed in 1958 - thirteen years after World War II ended and after the United States worked hand-in-hand with the communists in the Soviet Union together to end Hitler's dream.

Birchers assert that the U.S. government is controlled by a group of Satan-loving internationalists, bankers, Jews and corrupt politicians who seek a "one-world socialist government."[3] They believe that this will come about, gradually, through the decline in Western Civilization, but mostly, they believe that secret traitors in the United States will tear up the Constitution and, one day soon, hand over our sovereignty to the United Nations.[4] They believe that the United Nations was only created for one reason and that was to eliminate the United States of America from the face of the earth. I was warned that a "New World Order" was on its way, in which there would be no countries, no borders, no culture, one language, one currency, one military and we would be slaves to the one-world government known as the United Nations.

When I finally came to the same conclusion as Dad that we were the only real threat to stop the advance of communism in America, I was worried that the commies or our government would break into the Birch headquarters, steal the database and then start killing us all. Dad had the same concern, but was confident that the membership lists would never be released.

It was only a matter of time, Dad would constantly warn me, until America would cease to exist. The Bill of Rights, the Declaration of Independence and the Constitution would just be pieces of failed history. We'd all be slaves in a socialistic or Marxist state, or even worse, full-blown communist slaves!

The Communist Manifesto would be the country's new bible and the

United Nations' Declaration of Interdependence would be our new constitution. Religion would be illegal. Freedom of speech wouldn't exist. Our armed forces would be called Peace Keepers and they would be controlled by the United Nations. Gun ownership would be illegal. Everything I knew and loved about America would cease to exist.

"The global power elites view the UN as their main vehicle for establishing, step by step, a socialistic global government controlled by them," said Welch. "Now, more than ever, we need to get the US out of the UN and the UN out of the US." There have been hundreds and hundreds of billboards with this message on them all over America since the late fifties.[5]

To think that the UN only exists to enable the overthrow of America is ludicrous, foolish and, sadly, a very real story for millions of paranoid Americans including 2016 Republican Presidential candidate Ted Cruz. "What President Obama wants to do is, he's run to the United Nations and wants to use the United Nations to bind the United States and take away our sovereignty."[6]

The John Birch Society said the same thing about President Kennedy just before he was assassinated in 1963.[7]

This scenario is what drives Birchers crazy and kept me up late when I was a teenager. They ultimately believe that Satan is behind this war to destroy America and he's hiding inside the United Nations Headquarters in New York City. This war or New World Order would never end until the United States of America ceased to exist. Birchers see all of this as good versus evil, right versus wrong, white versus black, freedom versus slavery, and ultimately, God versus the Devil.

The Birch Society uses the illusion that we are all oppressed victims of evil (taxes, regulations, equality, immigration, foreign aid and gun control) and that our own government is out to control all aspects of our lives. I was taught that we were being persecuted for believing in the Constitution and for loving Jesus. Yet we had God and the Constitution on our side, and if we worked hard enough we would ultimately prevail in keeping America free. God loves America and our Constitution more than anything or anyone else. I believed all of this to be true.

The John Birch Society teaches that the American people are comprised of four groups: "communists, communist dupes or sympathizers, the uninformed who have yet to be awakened by the communist danger, and the ignorant."[8] Dad preached this and I judged my friends and teachers the same. Americans to me were either commies, liberals, dummies who didn't care or smart like us.

Going to college was never an option for me or my siblings and not just because my parents were poor and we didn't have good enough grades - it was to protect us "from the brainwashing which happens every day on every college campus in America," Dad would say.

Birchers believe that the Civil Rights Movement and the efforts of Martin Luther King Jr., Malcolm X, Jesse Jackson, Louis Farrakhan and others existed only to spread communism throughout America.[9] Dad said that greed was the major motivator behind civil rights and that black people were trying to take advantage of the system by fighting for more rights. Birchers live in a world of absolutes and singular focus. In their world, there is no middle-ground or opportunity for debate, consideration or rationalization.

The John Birch Society doesn't like the Metric System because America, if it relied on it like other countries, would be one step closer to the New World Order. All Birchers hate the Metric system because of this and the other theory that the Metric system is evil because the people who created it, the French, hate God.[10]

Birchers hate taxes, but they like smooth highways and want to have more nukes than the Russians and every other country on this planet combined. Dad warned that every nuke treaty ever created only existed for the purpose of disarming America. Dad said that treaties never benefited America. They only make us weaker according to him, because other countries would never disarm and we would be left unguarded.

Birchers believe fluoride in our drinking water will make us communists because they feared that the Soviets would put poison in our water systems.[11] They are opposed to sex education in public schools as well as all cultural and art issues. However, they are not opposed to Christmas trees in public places. Unless, of course, you call it an "Xmas" tree, which is also considered part of the Communist Conspiracy to have us quit using the word "Christmas" - an attempt to take "Christ" out of the holiday. It is interesting to note that the origins of the word "Xmas" date back to the 16th century.

Birchers would fight to the death or kill a doctor to prevent an abortion. In their view, any organization that supports human rights, animal rights or the environment is pro-communist. They reject the science of global warming, pollution and environmental regulations saying they are all created to destroy free enterprise and capitalism.

Birchers hate government. They hate what America has turned into today. Gay marriage, civil rights, a Martin Luther King Jr. federal holiday and public education are all signs to them that America is just about completely red and dead. They long for the day of a modern American life like what is portrayed in *Little House on the Prairie*. Birchers believe that there are communists in every element of our federal government. "Seventy to ninety percent of the responsible personnel in the Department of Health, Education, and Welfare are communists," said Welch.[12]

Like 2016 GOP Presidential candidate Rand Paul, the John Birch Society would like to eliminate the Departments of Education, Commerce, Energy and Housing along with Homeland Security, the IRS and the EPA among other agencies. Birchers believe that governments will always be in contempt of us and out to ruin our lives. "The greatest enemy of man is and always has been government. And the larger, the more extensive that government, the greater the enemy," said Welch.[13]

Birchers are no different than the young men being suckered in to join gangs. They feel helpless, lonely and angry. My dad fit this profile and sadly, even though he's been a member for over forty years now, he stills feels helpless, lonely and angry. Yet, once anyone is accepted among others of similar negative projections, they immediately feel justification in an almost sociopathic narcissistic way.

I know I did as I used to read the *New American* and other Birch material all the time. I knew things other people didn't. I was smarter, I thought. I was informed. I was right. I was a dedicated and conscious member of one of the most pathetic, embarrassing and ignorant organizations in America and I was proud! Everyone else I knew, except my dad, was stupid. I knew this to be true.

Robert Welch was the founder of the John Birch Society. He along with eleven other prominent and wealthy conservatives via Welch's exclusive invitation started this group. Welch created and named it after a fundamentalist Baptist missionary and American Military Intelligence Officer, John Birch who was killed by the Chinese communists within days after the end of World War II. The John Birch Society calls him the first casualty of the Cold War.

The Birch Society believes that the Chinese communists singled out Birch because of his "obsession with his fight against the increasing forces of evil in the world."[14]

In the book, *The Secret File on John Birch*, authors James and Marti Hefley detail that John's parents, knew that John, before leaving for China, had felt the greatest peril to world peace was international communism (even though we were partners with the communists to fight Hitler), not Japanese Imperialism or Hitler. A few weeks before the war ended, Birch had written a letter to his parents, "I believe that this war will set the stage for Antichrist. I'll have a lot to tell you when I get home - things about the future of China and the world."[15]

Disenchanted with what the military told them about their sons' death, his parents wondered if the Chinese killed him (John) because they felt he knew too much. They believed the Chinese wanted to prevent him from coming home because he was proclaiming that they were harboring the secret Antichrist.

Robert Welch was a gifted individual who was home-schooled by his mother. The University of North Carolina admitted him at the age of twelve. He later attended the U.S. Naval Academy and Harvard Law School, but dropped out of both because of the conflicts he had with many professors whom he accused of being communists.

Welch's company and one-man show, the Oxford Candy Company went out of business during the Great Depression. Welch later joined his brother John at his candy company, which brought the world Sugar Daddies, Sugar Babies and Junior Mints. He made a lot of money and retired a wealthy man in 1956. The company was sold to Nabisco in 1963.

Robert Welch ran for political office but never got elected. He spent a lot of his wealth on various causes other than the John Birch Society including supporting Joseph McCarthy's re-election campaign in 1952.

His robust leadership of the John Birch Society is well documented. The Society was his and the words he spoke were taken literally by the membership. If Welch said that Ewoks from *The Empire Strikes Back* were communist spies in cute little furry outfits - Bircher's would hate them and anything to do with Star Wars, George Lucas, Carrie Fisher, Harrison Ford, or R2D2. Movie theaters that played the movie would be boycotted and so on.

Welch stated that President Dwight Eisenhower was a dedicated, conscious agent of the Communist Conspiracy.[16] He stated that FDR knew Japan was going to bomb Pearl Harbor, but kept it a secret so we could go drop the A bomb on them.[17] Welch later backed-off of his accusations towards Eisenhower and said that he really didn't believe that Ike was a real communist, but rather he was a "dumb tool" unknowingly helping the communist cause.

The wealthy men who helped Welch create the John Birch Society also included an exceptionally rich man named Fred Koch. He is the father of the two sons who currently run Koch Industries (the second largest private corporation in the U.S. with annual revenue in 2014 of over $115 billion) and are involved in numerous extreme right-wing causes in America. Neither brother claims or admits to being a member of the Society presently, but Charles Koch (worth over $41 billion according to *Forbes*) was an avid Bircher with a lifetime membership and even opened a John Birch Society bookstore in Wichita, Kansas in the sixties. Both brothers are presently ranked in the top ten of the world's richest people.

Their father Fred was an oil man who in the late twenties worked with the communists in Russia and set them up with his modified version of "cracking" - a process in which crude oil is refined into gasoline.

Koch's story on how he ended up working in the Soviet Union provides a little insight into his paranoia and anger. In 1921, an engineer working for the Universal Oil Products Company in America developed an advanced version of cracking called the "thermal cracking process." Koch and his partner with their company, Winker-Koch Engineering Company, barely altered this version of the thermal cracking process and then sold these cracking stills throughout America. UOPC had patents on their thermal cracking process and they successfully sued Koch and shut his company down in the United States.

During this lawsuit, Koch, fed up with the lawsuit and the U.S. government for getting involved, focused his business efforts to the East and developed new relationships in the Soviet Union and the Middle East.

It was during this time, while in the Soviet Union, that Koch made many Russian friends. One of those friends, as described by Koch in his 29-page book, *A Business Man Looks at Communism*, was assigned to him by the Russian government to be his guide. This guide (Jerome Livshitz) "told me (Koch) how the communists were going to infiltrate the U.S.A. in the schools, universities, churches, labor unions, government, armed forces, and to use his words, 'make you rotten to the core.'"

Fred Koch not only helped create the John Birch Society, but was also instrumental in numerous attacks on labor, public education, civil rights and anything in America that he viewed as a threat to his wealth, philosophy and lifestyle. He wrote that "the colored man looms large in the Communist plan to take over America," and that public welfare was a secret plot to attract rural blacks and Puerto Ricans to Eastern American cities to vote for communist causes and ultimately in "getting a vicious race war started." He fought the civil rights movement and claimed that racial desegregation was a communist plot and would lead to a "mongrelization" of the races.[18]

Like Welch, Koch was severely extreme in his fear mongering towards the Communist Conspiracy. "Maybe you don't want to be controversial by getting mixed up in this anti-communist battle," Koch said in a speech to a Women's Republican Club in 1961. "But you won't be very controversial lying in a ditch with a bullet in your brain."[19]

The John Birch Society is notorious for printing and saying inflammatory and dangerous things. They lost a landmark libel lawsuit to Elmer Gertz, an attorney, after a fourteen-year battle that ended up in the Supreme Court. They had claimed he orchestrated a wrongful conviction and that he was a member of various communist front organizations.[20]

Throughout the years, the Society has blatantly attacked politicians, mainstream conservative organizations, conservative media outlets and even many conservative republicans for not being radical enough. They called them traitors. They called them communist sympathizers if they didn't consider them as anti-communist as the John Birch Society.[21]

William F. Buckley, largely known as the godfather to America's conservative movement for the past half century, has said the Birch Society was "so far removed from common sense," and dismissed the Society as dangerous to our Republic. He was so offended by Robert Welch and his John Birch Society that he ran a six-page editorial attacking them in his *National Review* in 1962, even though he knew it would alienate a lot of his readers and Birch members (including his own mother).

The FBI and J. Edgar Hoover described the Birch Society as "extremist," "irrational," "irresponsible," "fanatics," and "lunatic fringe."[22]

Even Ayn Rand, the famous libertarian, in an interview in *Playboy Magazine* said, "I consider the Birch Society futile, because they are not for capitalism, but merely against communism... No country can be destroyed by a mere conspiracy; it can be destroyed only by ideas. The Birchers seem to be either non-intellectual or anti-intellectual.[23]

The John Birch Society, despite their rhetoric, is not a pro-American organization. They're not specifically all Republicans or Democrats. They'll tell you that there are commies and traitors in both parties. They are a radical anti-government cult who embody and embrace fear and hate to maintain their false sense of patriotism. I know this to be true because I grew up in the John Birch Society where I learned fear, paranoia and hate as a way of life.

3. RUN TO THE HILLS

During first grade in 1975, we (my parents, younger sister and I) moved from California back to Western Washington. We lived in a used single-wide trailer situated just a few feet off of an old country road surrounded by hundreds, if not thousands of evergreen trees. The trailer was on my grandma's (Dad's mom's) property. Maybe fifty people lived down this road. The County operated a rock quarry just a few hundred yards down the hill from our house and at the end of the road, about two miles further, was a tree farm.

Grandma lived right next door to us in an old, rustic wooden cabin. We had no immediate neighbors otherwise and most every other house or trailer located off the road had a long muddy driveway so they weren't viewable. People kept to themselves in this part of the world. This style of living was a lot different from life in the San Fernando Valley where the Latino population dominated and there were houses and apartments everywhere.

One of the many reasons we moved to Washington was so Dad could be closer to his mom, who lived a very rural and independent lifestyle alone in the woods. Grandma gave my parents the land for their single wide trailer. A few years later, Grandma gave Dad and Mom even more land across the street and up the hill, where our standard of living was upgraded with a new double-wide trailer and the mortgage that came with it. A few years later, Grandma moved across from us and lived in the old single-wide trailer that we had earlier occupied.

We were a poor family compared to most of the other people in the area. We obviously weren't homeless poor and I never went to bed hungry. We were just barely getting by and certainly weren't getting ahead. Based on my perceptions of how my friends and their families lived, we were poor in my mind and rather trashy with how our yard and house looked. My friends' parents all had regular jobs, steady incomes and most of them lived in real stick-built houses.

From that time on we lived in the woods. The nearest grocery store or gas station was five miles away. I was the oldest child and by the time I was in third grade, I was big enough to help Dad with outside chores. We spent a lot of one-on-one time together.

Dad never held down a job with any consistency in the seventies except for a couple of years when he painted cruise missiles working for the Boeing Company. He boasted that the missiles he painted would one day kill some commies.

He got laid off from that job after a year or two during a massive reduction in their workforce. In the late eighties he worked for the federal government at Fort Lewis painting tanks and speed bumps for the Army.

Mom didn't work and when Dad wasn't working a full-time job, he did odd jobs painting houses or selling firewood to pay bills.

Every August, when it came to "back-to-school" shopping, we could afford to get me only one new pair of shoes. While other kids had cleats for baseball and hi tops for basketball, I had one pair of shoes and they had to last all year. As bad as I felt that I had it growing up, my little brother had it worse as he'd get the "hand-me-downs" from me when I outgrew my clothes and shoes.

Mom filled her role as the stay-at-home, clean the house and make dinner wife. When she wasn't cooking or cleaning she spent her time watching daytime soap operas and going through the daily newspapers cutting out coupons. Often she'd go to a newspaper rack or box and steal dozens of the Sunday edition, which always had the most coupons.

She'd do this later in the day "since it wasn't really like stealing as they would probably get thrown away anyway," she would say. She'd also go to the bulletin boards at various grocery stores and take more than enough rebate and manufacturer coupons.

My parents never saved any money nor did anything smart with any extra money they got their hands on, which happened only when Mom hit a jackpot of a few hundred dollars at bingo.

She was all about saving money and then using those savings to get away from Dad and us kids, almost every night, to run off and go play bingo. She'd go play three to four nights a week at various bingo halls in the area driving up to thirty miles some nights. Mom was an avid bingo player. At the halls, everyone knew who she was and they were all nice to her. Sometimes I went with her when I was old enough.

To this day, I have no memories of Mom and Dad hugging or kissing or showing any affection at all to each other. Dad was rarely present. He was living in constant fear that, one day soon we were all going to end up as commie slaves.

My impression was that Dad believed there was no point in making a good living, having a nice life or being a good husband or dad. His main role in life was fighting the conspiracy and preparing us for an inevitable invasion.

Additionally, if you're not that smart and not that good at anything, what's the point of having a great job since we're all going to either die or be living in a communist slave camp anyway?

When I started eighth grade, there were four of us kids in the house. We had a few pigs on our property and once they were big enough, Dad would take his Colt 45 out, put it against their forehead and pull the trigger. Together, we'd then load the dead pig in the back of his beat up Ford pickup truck and take it to the butcher to be processed. The pigs were always the lucky recipients of our daily food scraps.

Once a week, Dad and I would take his truck to the old cheese factory in town where we would fill up a couple fifty-five gallon steel drums with whey. Whey is a liquid byproduct from the cheese-making process and it stinks like rotten milk, only worse. The whey was free and the pigs loved it. I always changed my clothes and took a shower after we finished unloading the truck at home.

We didn't haul our trash to the local dump like everyone else who lived on our road. Instead, Dad would get on his tractor and find a place on our property that wasn't viewable from the driveway. He would dig a pit large enough to bury a full-size truck.

Every day, I'd throw all of our trash in it and then burn it. It would take a few years before the pit would fill up and then Dad would cover the pit with dirt. Then we'd repeat this process.

Every year, Mom and Dad would hide our Christmas presents in my grandma's tent camper, which she parked right next to her trailer (our old single-wide). One time, I snuck into the trailer to spy on the presents to see if I could figure out what I was getting. On top of the fold-out dining table, I saw a brown paper grocery bag that said "thirteen year-old boy" on it. In it were presents.

Those were my presents which my parents picked up from a local church in town. It was charity and we were the recipients. I felt bad when I saw that. My friends weren't getting their presents donated to them by a local charity. I felt embarrassed and was angry about this. I got socks. This was also the same Christmas that I figured out that there truly was no Santa. Even worse, we never attended the donating church.

Though my parents couldn't afford to buy us Christmas presents when we were young, Dad did decide to give money to the John Birch Society every month. He felt it necessary for every one of us to have our own memberships.

One benefit of being poor in America during this time was the opportunity to enjoy the sweet taste of government cheese that my parents brought home from the welfare office. This cheese was incredibly smooth and tasty. It never lasted long in the house. It was delicious. If you Google "seventies government cheese," you'll see I'm not alone with my adoration. "Government Cheese" even has its own Wikipedia page.

It was around eighth grade when I began to absorb and share in Dad's hatred for people and the world in general. This was about the time he began my educational training. He started talking to me like a young adult rather than a little kid.

Dad complained a lot about people taking advantage of the country. He said it was hurting good, hard-working Americans like us. He was angry and I was too. He said that too many people made more money on welfare every week than he did cutting firewood. Dad said most people were lazy, on drugs and wanted the government to take care of them. He was frustrated because according to him there were so many people on welfare that our taxes kept going up and there was no way we could get ahead.

Even though Dad was an angry person, he wasn't an overly punishing person who beat his kids a lot. This was the early eighties and spanking or hitting your kid with a paddle or a belt wasn't exactly frowned upon in his social circles. In fact, not hitting or spanking your kid was a sign of bad parenting.

I remember a night, however, when we had company at our trailer and Mom was telling me to do something. Like a typical mouthy twelve year-old, I guess, I talked back to her (just like Dad always did). I don't remember what I said to Mom, but within a second afterwards Dad grabbed me real hard by the back of my neck and told me to go outside and get a stick.

So I did.

I walked outside around our trailer and went to a cedar tree, grabbed a small branch about two feet long and brought it back to the front porch where he was waiting. Mom never came out.

He took the limb from me, stripped the needles and smaller branches off of it, told me to turn around and he whipped my backside with it three or four times. I cried, fell to the ground and begged him to stop.

He did and then threw the stick in the brush and walked back inside.

Another time, not too long after this (proving how effective whipping a child is), I was talking back to Mom again when Dad grabbed me, pushed me against the wall and punched me in the stomach. Mom screamed at him. I fell to the ground and Dad went outside.

I never did talk back to Mom again, at least not in front of Dad.

He always seemed to play rough whenever we'd wrestle around on the living room floor. He'd play dirty and his favorite moves were to jam a finger hard into my arm pit or push hard on my ear lobe with one finger which would cause serious sharp pain.

Dad always acted like we were having fun with this roughing around on the floor when I was a kid. And even though he weighed around 250 pounds and I wasn't even 100 pounds soaking wet, he'd get me on my back, pin me down, sit on my stomach and then he'd take his finger tips and pound on my sternum with a consistent sharp thump until the pain became unbearable.

Playing with Dad wasn't so much fun. In looking back, I realized, he wasn't interested in playing with me. Having kids who just wanted to play wasn't fun for him.

I played shortstop on the little league baseball team when I was twelve. Dad did show a little interest in helping me. I wanted to go to the park in town where we could play catch on the grass and Dad could hit ground balls to me. Instead, Dad would play catch with me at home where the ground was bumpy, muddy and had a lot of rocks and gravel everywhere. When the "infield groundout" came rolling at me, it was bouncing everywhere to the point where if I actually caught it, I was lucky. I think Dad enjoyed this nonsense, but it wasn't fun. He used to tell me that if I ever got good at stopping ground balls at home, I'd be real good at stopping them on a baseball field.

Dad did dedicate a fair amount of time and energy to encouraging me in hunting, archery and trapping. I'm guessing this was because he believed those two hobbies and skills might come in handy one day in a post-apocalyptic world. He would often take me to the archery range and buy me gloves and new arrows. He also put a lot of effort into buying various traps and showed me how and where to set them in the woods on the County's property next to ours.

Dad and I spent a lot of time together during these years. I was his first born after all, and unless you could help him with outside work, he had little use for you. My siblings were too young to help with the firewood.

Most days when I was in my preteen years, I'd get home from school and Dad would be waiting for me to help him load the firewood into his truck that he had cut during the day. We would go sell it to "yuppies," as he'd say. He was always nice to the yuppies in person, but talked crap about them behind their backs.

Often on our way back home if there was something on the side of the road, like a tire or a broken down car, Dad would turn around and investigate. Most times, he'd throw what he wanted in the back of the truck. One time, he jacked up a broken car and took the tires saying it was obvious the person who owned the car didn't care about it and probably abandoned it.

Other times, we'd drive behind the large grocery stores to the loading docks and pick up the used wooden produce crates.

We'd steal them and then take them to a local produce farm and sell them back. I use to get thirty-five cents for each crate from an old Japanese produce farmer who was always very nice to me. We'd get him a dozen or as many as we could load in the back of the truck on the way home. Dad said I could keep the money we received for selling the crates. That was my pay for helping and different from the "food, clothes and a roof over my head" lecture I received all the time.

Sometimes when Dad found a loaf of bread or a box of pastry treats in the dumpsters behind the grocery stores, he'd bring them home. If they weren't moldy or obviously spoiled, we'd eat them. Dad said the government made grocery stores throw away food that expired even though the food was still good and safe to eat. He said the government did this to hurt businesses.

Much of the time when Dad and I were in a place or at someone's house, and he saw a broken down vehicle, an old rusty storage tank, a stack of pallets, or whatever, he would inquire as to whether he could have it if they didn't want it. Most people didn't want this junk, he'd say, so we'd take it home. We lived on about forty acres with only about two or three acres actually level and cleared. Each and every day our property would expand with Dad's treasures. We were John Birch Society hillbillies.

4. AN IGNORANT MAN IS HALF AS DANGEROUS AS AN EDUCATED FOOL

The title of this chapter was the grand message I shared with all my classmates and teachers when I graduated from high school in 1986. I was so proud of this quote. It went right underneath my senior picture in our high school annual. It was my message - my good bye and a big middle-finger to everyone at school. Dad wanted me to use that quote in the school annual and I did. It wasn't mine. It was his. Dad made it up and was proud of me for using it.

The real message being delivered to my classmates and teachers was that it was okay to be a dumbass, rather than appreciating or continuing on with your education.

I was an idiot. I loved the quote. I was the ignorant man and all my friends headed to college were the educated fools. I thought that those who were going to college were dumb. I wanted to see the looks on their faces after each one of them read my quote. I wanted them to know that they were all stupid and I was smarter than them.

I have all of my high school annuals except the one from my senior year. I hid it underneath a drawer in my footlocker when I was at basic training in Fort Dix, New Jersey. I forgot it in the barracks when I left.

I've never seen my quote since, and sadly I'll never be able to get it out of my head. It's been thirty years since I graduated and I'm still embarrassed by it. I'm sure no one else cares or remembers. I wish I would have said something like, "we came, we saw and we kicked ass."

Because of how public education was presented to me by my parents, I had very little motivation for doing well.

There was no pressure to do well. The only pressure I felt was from Dad's message to be careful with the "education" they were trying to give me.

"Eighty-five to ninety percent of American children are still in the government schools, where they are being dumbed down and abused by the radical left who wants to turn them into liberal democrats," Robert Welch said in his *Blue Book*.

Not once, during high school was there ever a conversation with my parents about going to college. It wasn't an option.

College cost a lot of money and my parents couldn't afford that. Further, a college education was considered worthless and there was no chance that Mom, Dad or I would have been open to their "brainwashing" and then paying the bill for it.

Besides, the "communists have six thousand schools and colleges teaching political warfare, propaganda, agitation and subversion," That's what Welch wrote in his *Blue Book* in 1958. It was now 1986. I couldn't imagine how many more communists had infiltrated the college system in America. I certainly couldn't have done the math.

The public education system in America was a part of "the grand plan for the socialization of our country." According to Welch, "The history of the socialist movement in the U.S. is one of advocating mandatory public education. Recall that it's the tenth step toward communizing any country outlined by Karl Marx in *The Communist Manifesto*."

Dad said that our public education system was not in the Constitution and was un-American. Being a participant in this socialistic scheme was a struggle. There were plenty of days that I resented my teachers and classmates. I didn't understand why we were supporting this element of the conspiracy by going to a public school. It didn't make any sense to me.

Bringing good grades home wasn't important to either one of my parents. The purpose of going to school was only to get a high school diploma. I was warned to not pay attention to what my teachers were trying to teach me, but to pay enough attention to pass and graduate. Life would be easier if I had a high school diploma, Dad told me.

If Dad had his way (and he didn't), my brothers, sisters and I would have been home-schooled. That said, there was no way that either one of my parents would have been literate enough to have even followed a high school textbook. Not only that, Dad was too busy cutting down trees or working and Mom was too enthralled with her daytime soap operas to teach us anything. Neither one of them would have been interested enough to give up their day-to-day lifestyles for any of us kids. Besides, there was no free lunch at home for us proud Americans. The free lunches were at the public school and so we went.

I remember specifically not talking about the things at home that I had learned at school. No matter the topic, Dad was constantly irritated by us being at school except for the one year I took wood shop. He was happy that I took wood shop. Other than shop, there was no doing right since we weren't being educated about the things that Mom and Dad deemed important. I didn't talk to them about what happened at school unless I thought it would make them happy or proud. Usually I was wrong about this, as nothing ever really made them happy.

In the hallways between classes at school, I was the little nerd kid who had the back of his ears flicked by classmates and the older kids. I was picked on because I was different and very short (I was 4'9" in eighth grade) for my age. My haircut was a basic military haircut when long hair was popular.

Both Dad and I would get our hair cut (even though he was mostly bald) every month at a barbershop at the Old Soldier's Home, (a retirement facility for old soldiers, most from WWII). My hair was short - geeky military short, which wasn't cool at all at that time. It looked like it was from the forties. I had an old soldier's haircut and I was thirteen years old. It was a bad hair style that required combing from the left to the right and was maintained with a little hair gel – think Adolph Hitler's hairstyle - but shorter. Dad didn't care if I liked it or if the other kids made fun of me.

Even though we were living in the early eighties, our school was about five years behind the times so everyone wore clothes that were popular in the late seventies. I didn't. Mom picked out the clothes I wore. I would have looked normal if we were living in the late fifties or early sixties in small town America.

Dad liked how I looked - which was all that mattered even though I hated it.

I never did share with him or Mom the bullying that took place throughout junior high and my first couple of years in high school. This all happened before puberty finally kicked in during my junior year. I was obviously a depressed loner kid while most of the other kids were normal. They were all more accepted by each other than I was.

Other parents cared if their kids were happy and they wanted them to fit in with the rest of the kids. Mine said they couldn't afford popular clothes. Mom could afford to go to bingo four to five nights a week. Dad could afford to send the John Birch Society money and to buy more guns, but they couldn't afford to buy the right jeans or the right haircut or at least something that didn't make me look like a social reject.

I was mocked by some of my friends, as they called me "virgin boy" in front of other people and even girls. It was embarrassing and hurtful as they had girlfriends and I didn't even like girls yet. I had little knowledge of the birds and bees and had never even seen a *Playboy* or naked girl before I was fourteen. I had no idea how sex worked or why, and in my mind, "screwing" meant that my penis worked like a cork screw and I'd have to spin around on top of a girl to have "sex." There was absolutely no talk in regards to these matters at home and sex education wasn't in the school's curriculum in the early eighties. A year later, I discovered Dad's *Penthouse* and *Hustler* magazines underneath his bed. Though not exactly comparable to teenage girls, I was able to connect the dots on how most things worked on the human body after studying those magazines.

Before I discovered *Penthouse* and *Hustler*, I accidentally called a "living organism" a "living orgasm" during my ninth grade biology class. Everybody, including the teacher, laughed really loud. I didn't know why my classmates and teacher were laughing at me at the time, but I was embarrassed and confused. I didn't know what the word "orgasm" meant. It was a simple mistake and one that humiliated the crap out of me the next day before school when I asked a classmate what an orgasm was.

Dad bought me my two favorite t-shirts at the Western Washington Gun Show when I was in ninth grade. They were both black. One said "Kill 'em All, Let God Sort 'em Out" and the other said "Better off Dead than Red." I wore them to school all the time. The "Kill 'em All" shirt had an attack helicopter on it spraying bullets and rockets into a jungle and the "Better off Dead" shirt had a fully-armed bald eagle on it that was draped in an American flag. I loved those shirts and I wore them all the time. Dad had the same two shirts.

I was an avid reader of *Soldier of Fortune* magazine during this time. Dad introduced me to the magazine and would buy it for me often.

Inside were glorious stories of the heroes and patriots who'd kill anyone (but mainly communists) to keep America free - for a fee. These guys were willing to die or kill to keep America free and they were getting paid a lot of money to do this. The magazine was always with me at school and at home.

My favorite part of the magazine, in addition to the stories about killing and how much money they got paid, were the classified ads in the back where different entities or people were looking to hire mercenaries. There were opportunities within this exciting career field of keeping America free. Not only was it exhilarating imagining that I might actually have a career of killing people (hopefully commies) and getting paid good money, but I'd also be a great patriot like my dad.

In 1983, the film *Uncommon Valor* came out starring Gene Hackman and Patrick Swayze. The movie was about a group of guys who went to Laos in the eighties to rescue a prisoner of war (POW) who had been imprisoned there for over a decade. Most of the men were former buddies of the POW, but one of them (Swayze) was a young stud and I idolized his character and role. I wanted to be just like him and go over there to help rescue other POW's too. This movie along with *Soldier of Fortune* gave me inspiration and hope in knowing that one day I too would be able to make a difference in the world and make Dad proud.

My career choice in 1984 was one that was unfamiliar to my teacher. My teacher (Dad and I were certain he was a card-carrying member of the Communist Party) didn't like it. I didn't care. While my classmates were selecting career fields in law enforcement, education, farming, engineering and so on, my dedicated passion and my choice of career was to become a mercenary - a professional who would kill people for money.

This was during my sophomore year in my "careers" class. The point of the careers class was to allow the student the chance to start thinking about college and/or a career after high school

The class required more than just a career choice or college degree selection. We had to write a lengthy report on what we wanted to do, why, how, and where. My report was over a dozen pages, and in it, I discussed the pros and cons of killing people for money and the type of training that would be necessary.

I did have limitations. I was certain that I'd never be able to kill a true patriot or a good American, of course – no matter how much money I was offered. Dad was happy. My teacher wasn't. I got a C- on my report. My future was set. Dad, as you can imagine, was incredibly proud of me. He was touched. I made him so happy with this project; I was thrilled. We were very close after this for a while. We were always very close for a short while after I did something to prove my loyalty to him and the cause. I was on my way to becoming Dad's right-hand man in the war against the Communist Conspiracy. I was happy.

I was fourteen when I wrote my first letter to the editor of the local newspaper. The purpose in this was to correct the editorial board of the

Tacoma News Tribune in regards to what form of government we had in the United States. Consistently, this newspaper and others used the word "democracy" and that was bad. I was taught democracies can lead to dictatorships and we Americans were being duped by the media. The United States was a "republic" – a government based on the principals of laws.

Robert Welch said that "newspapers write ringing editorials declaring that this is and always was a democracy." My letter was published in the newspaper. I was convinced the Editorial Board and all of their readers now knew the truth.

I took a copy of that edition of the *Tribune* to school and showed the letter to my friends. You can imagine how awesome my sophomore classmates thought I was. I glowingly showed it to most of my teachers as well. I was that kid.

The motivation for writing that letter was, of course, to appease Dad and do my part in saving America. Writing letters to media outlets and elected officials was also our duty as members of the John Birch Society. Not only that, the published letter was heartfelt for me. I was deeply concerned about the future of America. I was incredibly proud that my letter was published. For at least that day, I had hope for the Republic.

In President Reagan's "State of the Union" speech on January 25, 1983, he said, "last year, I announced the commitment of the United States to developing the infrastructure of democracy throughout the world. We intend to pursue this democratic initiative vigorously. The future belongs not to governments and ideologies which oppress their peoples, but to democratic systems of self-government which encourage individual initiative and guarantee personal freedom."

After we heard this, we were horrified. Our fear was that Reagan was abandoning ship and trying to turn the world into a democracy and then eventually a dictatorship. This fear, over such trivial debate, exists only because of Welch's paranoid conspiracy theories. Reagan's traitorous speech was my immediate motivator for writing the letter.

Isaac Asimov, the famous author and professor once said that "there is a cult of ignorance in the United States, and there has always been.

This anti-intellectualism has been nurtured by the false notion that democracy means that my ignorance is just as good as your knowledge."[1]

Dad would call Asimov a commie bastard.

Anti-intellectualism and anti-rationalism were the norms in my parent's house. "Anti-intellectual" is partly defined as "a person who believes that intellect and reason are less important than actions and emotion in solving problems and understanding reality." This explains the contempt and hatred we had for people who had evil "white collar" jobs. We hated those people. They weren't good people and they didn't want to really work for a living, Dad would say. They were snobs who didn't care about people who weren't white collar. "They have no idea what hard work is," he'd say. Dad said those people were unable to use common sense. They were fools with too much education to understand basic concepts and realities that were necessary to get through life.

For example, Dad explained that when stacking split firewood, the bark side should go face up to keep water off of the meat part of firewood. I used to wonder what the point of a "higher education" was, if you didn't even know how to stack firewood correctly?

At the time, I was quite confident that everything I needed to know in life was being taught to me by my father. Another thing he taught me (which I'm finally starting to realize isn't true), is that when you get hurt, like if you step on a nail, the way to control the pain was to bite your finger until the pain in your foot went away. You can mitigate the pain in your finger but not in your foot was his reasoning. It's this basic premise for problem solving that Dad applied to all areas in life. I did the same for many years. Had my high school teachers taught me good stuff like this, Dad would have approved of the public education I received.

The real coup of my high school experience took place my sophomore year during class officer elections in the spring for our junior year.

I was friendly with most of the cliques in my class. Not all of them were jerks or bullies. There were maybe 25-30 kids in my grade. Anyway, for the election, I was running to become class president. Yes, a hostile takeover was imminent. Most of the kids who were class president types were smart - the 4.0 kids. I was more of a 3.0 kid with little chance that the 4.0 kids who always went to the class meetings would ever vote in a 3.0 kid for class president.

My plan was simple. I needed to get a few non-4.0s to the class meeting where the vote would take place. If I could recruit new voters, I'd win.

All it took was three of my friends to come to their first class meeting and vote. They did and I won. The next year I went on to become junior class president. My coup was a success! The 4.0 kids weren't thrilled about my victory at all. I sensed their resentment. I didn't care. When I told my parents they didn't even care that I had won. I didn't really feel anything when they didn't respond because this was normal for them.

5 SUMMERTIME BLUES

When I was fifteen years-old, my parents sent me away to the John Birch Society summer camp located at the YMCA campgrounds in Lake Wenatchee, WA. The camp lasted for a week and was filled with many hours of lectures, slide shows and recreational activities like hiking, canoeing and volleyball. The purpose of a Birch Society summer camp, of course, was to educate young Americans regarding the impending communist threat lurking over America. Every day, there were nearly a dozen educational programs or classes as well as the normal camp activities you'd expect including nightly campfire sing-a-longs.

I hated the camp and on day two after crying on the phone to Mom for what seemed like hours, Dad packed up and drove over five hours, picked me up and reluctantly took me home. It wasn't necessarily the camp that I hated as much as I hated not being at home. I was homesick.

The prior year, my parents sent me to a Baptist church camp. I didn't make it through the first night there either after being homesick.

When I was sixteen and mostly through puberty (and nearly six feet tall now), they sent me back to Birch Camp. This time, I not only survived and lasted through the entire week, I thrived at camp. I was extremely familiar with the subject matter. This was the same subject matter that Dad was putting in my head all the time. I knew that Alger

Hiss was a commie and a traitor when he conspired with other members of the illuminati to create the United Nations. I knew that Kissinger was a traitor and the same went for Nixon and Reagan. I knew that they were trying to kick Jesus and God out of school so I would worship Satan. I knew that the government wanted to implant a microchip in me to control my brain and know my location at all times. I knew a lot of the stuff that the instructors were talking about - I was the perfect Birch camper.

Besides, there was a pretty girl from Oregon, who showed a keen interest in me. She made camp even more fun as we'd sneak out of our respective cabins at night and meet down by the lake to hang out.

Birch Camp was everything one could pretty much imagine it would be, based on the name "John Birch Society Summer Camp." Every instructor was an old white guy preaching about topics including how we needed to get the United States out of the United Nations, how the liberal media lies to us, how our high school teachers try to brainwash us, why civil rights is a lie, and the debate tactics of liberals and other conspiracy theories, (which weren't called conspiracy theories).

Camp was an absolute reassurance of what I had been taught at home by Dad. Everything that I knew to be the "truth" was confirmed by these other men at camp with their speeches and reading materials.

I sat up front during all the lectures. I raised my hand often to answer questions and to ask questions. I sang out loud during the campfire sing-a-longs. I had even borrowed an acoustic guitar from one of the counselors and played it in front of dozens of other campers and counselors. I didn't know how to play it at the time, but my self-confidence was so high that I wasn't afraid of much.

"Over hill, over dale,
We will hit the commies trail,
As we Birchers, go marching along."

Not only did I excel in the course material and topics, I was really popular with my fellow campers and completely in my element at Birch

Camp. I was cool. Cool like James Spader in *Less Than Zero* and cool like C. Thomas Howell in *Red Dawn*. I was finally excelling at something. This was the first time in my life when I knew I was cool and smart. It felt great! The kids liked me and even the speakers and instructors liked me as I showed a tremendous amount of interest in the classes. I was finally popular.

Apparently I was even more popular at camp than I had realized.

In 2013, I received emails from two separate women whom I don't remember at all from camp. One of them saw my name somewhere, found my email address and they both sent me emails asking how I was. They shared that they both had big crushes on me at Birch camp.

One wrote "It is so funny how even after almost...I hate to say this...after 30 years some things really stick with you." Indeed, they do.

I think most kids at Birch Camp were sent by their parents so they could learn more about the world from the Birch perspective to counteract the education that they were likely receiving from school.

Birch Camp for me wasn't like school. It was a refresher course. I was already well-versed in the Conspiracy, the Illuminati, the Rockefellers, the Council on Foreign Relations, the Trilateral Commission, the United Nations, the International Monetary Fund, the World Bank, the Federal Reserve, the Warren Commission, the insiders, the establishment, Jews, the New World Order, etc. I had studied the U.S. Constitution, the Declaration of Independence, the Bill of Rights, Welch's *Blue Book*, Chairman Mao's *Little Red Book*, and Karl Marx's *The Communist Manifesto* (It's important to know how the enemy thinks). I was the perfect John Birch Society summer camp kid. I was the future of the John Birch Society and I was going to be a leader in this revolution that would save America. I could have almost run the camp myself I thought.

My favorite book at Birch Camp wasn't the Bible. It was Welch's *Blue Book* and in it there was a quote that I had memorized and could recite to you at any time in the mid-eighties. "Lenin died in 1924. But before he died he had laid down for his followers the strategy for this conquest. It was, we should readily admit, brilliant, farseeing, realistic and majestically simple. It has been paraphrased and summarized as follows. 'First, we will take Eastern Europe. Next, the masses of Asia. Then we shall encircle the last bastion of capitalism, the United States of America. We shall not have to attack; it will fall like overripe fruit into our hands.'"

I knew this quote as well as the Pledge of Allegiance.

Welch's words were quoted in the *Blue Book* to engage the reader to take action and to instill a sense of purpose and rage. The *Blue Book* was my bible. It was filled with what I and others perceived as the truth even though it was simply written by one man as his own opinion and vision. Lenin's quote scared the heck out of me and it fueled my paranoia.

In 1985, President Reagan repeated Lenin's exact quote when asked by the *New York Times* if he thought that the Soviet Union was still an "Evil Empire."

During the writing of this book, however, I tried to track down exactly when Lenin had said this. The *New York Times* checked with the Library of Congress and there's no record of this speech ever existing. They checked *The Collected Works of Lenin* and it's not there either. They eventually tracked it down in the book *None Dare Call it a Conspiracy* (published by the John Birch Society of course in 1971) and it quotes Robert Welch's *Blue Book* as the source of the quote.

"So there it is: an undocumented Birchite 'paraphrase' offered 'often' as a live quotation by a President of the United States," concluded the editorial in the *Times*.

Welch made up the Lenin quote. It wasn't real. I had memorized a fake quote and had believed it to be true until October 2015. The founder of the John Birch Society was a liar. I was an idiot. Duh.

My parents did not pay me for me to go the John Birch Summer Camp. Every year, Bob Chipp, Washington State Director of the John Birch Society, would go to various Birch meetings throughout the state and ask members to help send a teenager to Birch Camp. Cost was $150 to go. Members would contribute money so some poor white Bircher's kid could go to camp. That was me - son of a poor white Bircher man.

The John Birch Society Summer Camp program was started in 1970 and ran until 2009 after it could no longer afford to keep the program afloat.[1] They tried to hand it off to other sister organizations a few times before finally killing it in 2009. Every year since its inception, though, nearly 1,000 kids from all over America were sent to various Birch Camps to learn about the Conspiracy. As Robert Welch said, "For truth in the hands and minds of youth becomes a doubly powerful weapon."[2]

The Society hasn't abandoned the concept of brainwashing children. They are providing "Judeo-Christian values" and a "classic American curriculum" by supporting parents with online courses they can obtain so they can brainwash their children at home.[3]

6 NONE DARE CALL IT A CONSPIRACY

When I was a very young member of the radical right in 1983, U.S. Congressman Larry McDonald was killed, when the plane on which he was a passenger was shot down by the Russians.[1]

McDonald was now the National Chairman of the John Birch Society and a Democratic Congressman from Georgia.[2]

Korean Air Lines Flight 007 was a scheduled flight from New York to Seoul, Korea and was carrying 269 passengers. Sixty-one of them were Americans and one of them in many minds was the most important man on the planet. "He (McDonald) was the most principled man in congress," said Ron Paul.[3] He was also the relatively new chairman of the John Birch Society having taken over that role less than six months prior in March 1983 after Welch died.

"There is a real question in my mind that the Soviets may have actually murdered 269 passengers including sixty-one Americans and crew on the KAL Flight 007 in order to kill Larry McDonald," said Jerry Farwell, the American pastor and co-founder of the Moral Majority.[4]

The plane was shot down after it accidentally crossed over into Soviet airspace. To this day, there are thousands of Americans who believe that the plane was shot down intentionally by the Russians to murder McDonald because of the threat he posed to the Communist Conspiracy.

I used to believe this as well and that night, on the news, when we found out about this, I knew that World War III had begun.

McDonald was cut from the same ideological cloth as Welch and Koch.

In 1975 McDonald said, "The drive of the Rockefellers and their allies is to create a one-world government combining capitalism and communism, under the same tent, all under their control... Do I mean conspiracy? Yes, I do. I am convinced there is such a plot, international in scope, generations old in planning, and incredibly evil in intent."[5]

McDonald's widow claims it was no accident that her husband was killed by the Russians.[6] Other theorists claim that McDonald knew too much about the evil workings of the Reagan Administration and that along with the CIA, FBI and Russia, they all conspired to have the plane blown out of the sky.

Larry Flynt, of *Hustler* fame, went as far as buying a full-page advertorial in the *Chicago Tribune* later in 1983 and in it, suggested that McDonald and the Birch Society, Reagan and the CIA were all in on the murder together in an attempt to boost America's efforts in the arms race. "A man like McDonald was so nuts that his martyrdom cannot be ruled out as a motive. In his world, the sacrifice of 268 other people would have been nothing compared to eliminating the 'incomparably greater evil' of communism," said Flynt.[7]

Others (including many Birchers) believed that the plane was never actually shot down, but instead was escorted to Russia where the passengers have been enduring a life of slavery in a KGB prison somewhere in "one of the Soviet Middle Asian Republics."[8]

Jessie Helms, the late Republican Senator from North Carolina, subscribed to this theory when he wrote a letter to Russian President Boris Yeltsin in which at the end of it, he requested answers to the numerous questions including these two:

1. "How many KAL-007 family members and crew are being held

in Soviet Camps?"

2. "Please provide a detailed list of the camps containing live passengers and crew, together with a map showing their location."

Helms sent this letter on official United States Senate letterhead on December 10th, 1991 - over eight years after the incident. And, for over eight years, a high-ranking United States Senator believed in this conspiracy. Yeltsin responded to all of the questions regarding the shooting down of the plane, but ignored the questions about the crew and Soviet camps.[9]

We were up in arms over the murder of McDonald. I was only fourteen years-old and the horrors of what I had been told all long by Dad appeared to be coming true. Dad said that this was the beginning of the end. We worried that our own government was going to break into the Birch Society headquarters and get the membership lists.

He believed that this murder of Larry McDonald was the start to a violent end of America.

Dad also knew of the "Form 4473" which he believed our own government would hand over to the communists. The form was a list of all American citizens who owned guns. This was the same form that the Cuban general asks for in the movie *Red Dawn*, so his soldiers could go collect all the guns and imprison the gun owners.

"Suppose there comes a time when a dictator takes over or a leader surrenders our nation. A dictator or foreign conqueror would love to have information on gun ownership. A tyrant would also like to take the IRS intact because of all the information held on Americans," the *New American*.[10] We were smart though. Dad never registered his guns so they wouldn't know about us.

I was really worried during this time, but we felt that we were prepared for whatever might happen. "Better dead than red," Dad would say. I kept thinking that maybe we should quit the Birch Society and hide in the woods. Honor was very important to Dad, however, as was being an anti-communist and a member of the John Birch Society. The thought of quitting the Birch Society out of fear was cowardly, he said. "Freedom was worth dying for."

Dad and I were outraged over the murder of McDonald. We were livid. We were both sure he was murdered and knew that Reagan would do nothing about it. "This should be war!" I'd say. I wanted World War III to happen. I wanted to drop a nuke on Russia and end communism for good.

Reagan's response to the murders was petty. "It was an act of barbarism," he said. "Our immediate challenge to this atrocity is to ensure that we make the skies safer and that we seek just compensation for the families of those who were killed."[11]

His remarks and complete lack of action was expected and disappointing. The leader of the John Birch Society and the most important member of the United States Congress had just been murdered by the communists and nothing was going to be done about it.

I was scared to death of what was going to happen next. It seemed like the end was near and there was no way out of this. Surely the U.S. had to respond. I was completely devastated. The Russians had killed the most important anti-communist man in the world and our government was going to do nothing about it.

This was arguably the tensest moment during the cold war and I wanted blood. I hated the communists. I feared them. They scared the hell out of me. This was Russia's first strike and I believed the United States needed to respond. Instead, an investigation was launched.

Russia apologized and said it was an accident. They said they thought the plane was on a spy mission. They simply apologized. All was forgiven by the United States.

In our minds and in the minds of thousands of others, this nonresponse or nonsense clearly meant that the United States government, the United Nations, Korea and likely even Japan were all working together with the Evil Russian Empire, hand in hand, to assassinate the leader of the John Birch Society. They needed to kill him and all the members of the John Birch Society for the conspiracy to be successful. It was exactly what Welch had stated back in 1976.

"But this is no creampuff war we are in, and the stakes involved are not those of a pillow fight. We have to face squarely up to the solid truth - that unless we are willing to take drastic steps, a lot of them, and very drastic indeed, we haven't a chance in the world of saving our lives, our country and our civilization. And we might as well start reconciling ourselves to having our children - not just our grandchildren - live under the Kremlin's rule, as Mr. Khrushchev indirectly prophesied."[12]

This was the time when nuclear annihilation was not only a very real possibility; it was constantly on my mind. Reagan consistently referred to the Soviets as the "Evil Empire" (before and after the shooting down of KAL Flight 007) and movies like *Rambo* (1982), *War Games* (1983) and *Red Dawn* (1984) had a serious influence on my reality. I wasn't only getting propaganda from Dad, the John Birch Society and *Soldier of Fortune* - I was getting it from popular mainstream movies too.

This paranoia was now even on the news as every day there were reports on the tensions between the U.S. and Russia. Of course it was all real and now the leader of the resistance, the leader of saving America from the commies, had just been murdered by them - most likely with help from my own government!

It's a good thing that I was only fourteen during this time. If I could have driven and had a car, I'm confident that my gun and I would have fought back by more than just going to another Birch Society meeting.

7 A DEAD LIBERAL IS A GOOD LIBERAL

"I tell people don't kill all the liberals. Leave enough so we can have two on every campus - living fossils - so we will never forget what these people stood for." - Rush Limbaugh, *Time Magazine*, 2001.

It was 1984. I was a teenager now and nothing had changed at home. Dad would get enraged when a leftist liberal appeared on our television in the living room. If Ed Asner, Jane Fonda, Barbra Streisand, Walter Cronkite, Cher or Alan Alda popped up on the TV, he would rage and yell, "Get those goddamn liberals off my TV!" I'd get up, or Mom or my sister would get up to turn the channel. Dad wouldn't get up. Sometimes Mom would tell him to knock it off and then he'd get up, turn off the television, then go outside - it didn't matter if we were all watching something. It was his TV and his behavior was the same in the eighties as it was in the seventies.

Showing non-white people on television was considered part of the conspiracy as were shows that Dad would call, "un-American."

He said the programmers at the television stations created shows that would soften us up to eventually become liberals. He believed that the *Cosby Show* existed so we would view black people as normal Americans. This show was quite a bit different from the black people that we had seen on *Sanford and Son, What's Happening* and *Fat Albert*.

The *Mary Tyler Moore Show* showed a career woman who didn't have children or a husband and that was wrong and promoted the Equal Rights Amendment. Watching that show, according to Dad, would lead us to supporting feminism and would ultimately be the complete destruction of the American family and the American way of life.

M.A.S.H. supposedly tried to make us accept homosexuality and gays in the military.

To Dad, all of these shows existed to brainwash us, to make us less American, more diverse and open-minded. He had programmed me to hate all of these shows. Like him, I feared that they were bringing about change in America that would one day lead us all to become socialists.

Dad hated all Hollywood leftists and most celebrities except a rare few (John Wayne, Clint Eastwood, Andy Griffith and Mel Gibson). Anyone who showed compassion or was for open transparency in society was a traitor and didn't deserve to live as far as he was concerned.

Dad explained that the reason most of the country's top celebrities would embrace liberalism and then communism was because those celebrities were promised immunity – a special life and place within the new system of government for them, their families and close friends in the new America. They wouldn't have to be slaves like the rest of us. These Hollywood liberals believed that the coming change was inevitable and if they didn't want to end up being slaves or have their children be slaves, they needed to help with the cause. The same was true for all the liberal politicians and democrats who were also promised a special role in the new America or the New World Order.

In the New World Order, those celebrities, wealthy liberals and the politically-connected would always have good food, clothing, nice homes, luxury items and more as long as they didn't rock the boat, Dad explained. "Actors have no talent other than to play pretend," he'd say. It wasn't hard for American celebrities to convince the masses that communism was a good thing. They were so good at pretending and most people were stupid, they'd believe them, he preached.

In Gary Allen's *None Dare Call it Conspiracy*, he states, "the one thing I can never figure out is why all these very, very wealthy people like the Kennedys, the Fords, the Rockefellers and others are for socialism. The idea that socialism is a share-the-wealth program is strictly a confidence game to get the people to surrender their freedom to an all-powerful collectivist government. While the insiders tell us we are building a paradise on earth, we are actually constructing a jail for ourselves."

John McManus, the third President of the Birch Society did clarify exactly what the conspiracy's plan was in his foreword to the 24th Printing of Welch's *Blue Book* in 1992. "Many of those who labored within this conspiratorial apparatus were working diligently to change America and drive her into the grip of totalitarian socialism. They still are. Their tactics include bribing the people with their own money, employing the use of force, deception and fear, and using every other trick they can think of to acquire total government power over the lives and well-being of the American people."

The Rockefellers, the illuminati and the insiders needed our land and our people to be their slaves. They persuaded or paid the media, the government and celebrities to convince us that liberalism, humanism, environmentalism and secularism was good. Then, in no time we'd all be red. Dad believes this. He taught me this and I believed him.

Like most Vietnam War Veterans, Dad harbors a deep hatred for Jane Fonda. He said she was supporting the communists in Vietnam and spit on American soldiers and led antiwar rallies when they returned home from Vietnam. She was a traitor. She needed to die. Like Dad, I wanted her dead.

We had many discussions about the traitors in America whether it was Fonda, Ted Kennedy, Jimmy Carter and others. If something really bad happened in America, like if Marshall Law was imposed or even if I got really sick and was told that I was terminally ill, I'd have to do something to make a change before I died. Dad said it was only a matter of time before there wouldn't be any states or America as a whole left anyway.

There was no way I would allow Jane Fonda to live in her communist utopia where she would be treated like a queen knowing what she did to my Dad, his fellow soldiers and all of America. I would take her out. I'd kill her and I'd be the best son ever and a damn fine patriot. "I'd be a national hero," I used to think. "Dad would be proud."

This was my back-up plan at the time in case I was dying or shit was about to hit the fan. I waited for the opportunity.

These thoughts were present in my mind in the early eighties. I never thought about blowing up government buildings or schools. But killing Fonda and Tom Hayden was something I would've certainly done if it was asked of me. That said, had Dad put a plan in my head to blow up an airport or a government building back then, there's no doubt in my mind that I would have done it. I would have done anything to make him proud of me.

When I recall the rage I had towards Fonda and how ridiculously evil my thinking became while I was under Dad's mind-control; the images of young suicide bombers in the Middle East pop up in my mind. They were convinced by their fathers or mentors to fulfill their destiny. These children are martyrs, which is what I could have been. It makes me sick.

The thought of living life as a communist slave was overwhelming. It was a constant source of anxiety and concern. It was horrible. I would have rather died than have to live in a world like that. My imagination ran wild with what it would be like to be a communist slave. It would have been like hell in my mind. Dad and I were on the same page - our psycho paranoid page.

It's a good thing that nothing medically terminal ever happened to me. I had always known that at some point, a doctor would tell me I have thirty days to live because of an illness. Little would that doctor know that by telling me that, he would've given Jane Fonda a death sentence.

And let's say that I did go on a killing spree and Jane Fonda and a few other commies ended up dead. What would Dad say about this and me? What would the Birch Society and every other right-wing extremist organization say about me and these inane acts? Would they have supported me and my acts of patriotism? Would I have been a hero to them? Would they say that I was framed or mentally ill?

What I don't understand and what still fuels my anger, however, is a childhood in which my dad provided inspiration and direction for scenarios in which it would be okay for me, as a fourteen year-old John Birch Society kid, to murder "un-American" people for patriotic revenge and glory. Mom says she wasn't aware of any of this and that my "dad was a good dad who tried his best."

Sure, there are many stories of extremely paranoid losers who have gone on killing sprees in America. It's another when a paranoid right-wing loser who's married with four kids spends his energy corrupting and brainwashing his firstborn to believe that if he was a good son and a good American, he'd go kill Jane Fonda when called upon. And I would have.

Dad raised me in his own despicable image with no moral compass whatsoever. I was constantly afraid the communists would take over the country and eventually the entire planet until there was no freedom and people wouldn't have their guns or happiness. There would be a one-world government with one currency, one language, one ruler, no borders and no America. What would the point be of living if I couldn't be an American, I often wondered?

The concept of killing a liberal to make America a better and safer place isn't something new. It's something that the extreme right-wing media has been suggesting now for quite some time.

"Hang on, let me tell you what I'm thinking. I'm thinking about killing Michael Moore, and I'm wondering if I could kill him myself, or if I would need to hire somebody to do it. No, I think I could," said Glen Beck, live on the "Glen Beck Program," in May 2015.

"I say round liberals up and hang 'em high. When I hear someone's in the civil rights business, I oil up my AR-25," said radio host Michael

Savage.[1]

These two guys are wildly popular right-wing radio hosts in America today who are adored and followed by millions.

Dad and I not only discussed killing people, we also celebrated the deaths of liberals or communists whenever they happened.

Dad often talked about how great it was that JFK was murdered. He said he deserved it for what he did in Cuba with the Bay of Pigs and for being a traitor and a commie. He also celebrated the death of Senator Edward Kennedy in 2009. "It's a good day when a Kennedy dies," I recall him saying. He even called my cell phone to share with me his good news about the late senator. Dad was thrilled when John Lennon was murdered. He said that Lennon deserved to die for saying he was bigger than Jesus.

8 IT'S THE END OF THE WORLD AND I KNOW IT

When we were "prepping" in the eighties, it wasn't called prepping. It was called getting your shit together for the day when a jeep full of commie soldiers came up the driveway looking to take us away or kill us if we resisted. They might be UN soldiers, US soldiers, Russians, Cubans - it didn't matter who it was.

We'd fight to the death to protect our property and our freedom. Dad prepared me for this scenario when I was a teenager. One method of my preparation involved me lying face down in the prone position in our wet and muddy gravel in front of our old double-wide trailer. In my hands was one of Dad's converted, full-auto AR-15's. It was loaded, and the excited warning coming out of his mouth was, "Russian Jeeps coming up the driveway!" That meant pull the trigger.

"Kill 'em all! Kill 'em all!" he yelled.

In my imaginative mind, I was aiming at the driver's side of the windshield trying to shoot the driver in the face. After I killed him, I'd look to the left waiting for the passenger to jump out and then I'd kill him too. This was the routine in my mind on how the first jeep battle would go down.

Dad always asked if I killed them all. I said I did and the 30 round bullet clip was now empty. Dad was happy. And so was I.

I was prepared for this attack. In me, Dad had created a fellow soldier to assist him with the impending invasion and fight. We figured that most Americans would probably roll over and turn red.

We wouldn't. "Better dead than red" he would say.

Growing up in the early eighties was a strange time for a young teenager scared to death of a soviet invasion, a nuclear war or even worse - the constant fear of being a communist slave in my own country.

"If we do not wake up to the real facts fast, and wake up enough of our fellow citizens, it will be our children and ourselves living as enslaved subjects of the Kremlin - possibly within five years, and certainly within ten to fifteen years at the very most. The danger is present, and it is very clear." This was all very real to me and this was written by Robert Welch in his *Blue Book* in 1958. Dad would often say the only reason we weren't slaves yet was because of the hard-working membership and leadership of the John Birch Society.

Dad was at this time a chapter leader in the John Birch Society. People were actually listening to him and supporting the cause. Dad didn't just talk Bircher propaganda to people. He'd also talk about guns, prepping and survivalist strategies.

Because of the rural area that we lived in, guns were very common and most people owned one or twenty. The fear that our government was going to repeal the second amendment and come take away our guns has, for well over half a century now, kept many paranoids stockpiling them - only because they fear that one day our government will try to confiscate all privately-owned guns in America.

In addition to working with Dad cutting firewood or going to John Birch Society Speaker events, we'd go to as many gun shows as possible.

I was too young to buy a gun at the gun shows. But instead of spending what money I had on junk food, candy or cassette tapes like my friends, I was buying water purification tablets, used army fatigues, ninja stars, and knives. I bought books on how to make homemade bombs and how to kill someone and make it look like a suicide. Dad was proud of my spending choices.

More than anything, at these guns shows, I was in the company of other informed patriots who knew that something really bad was going to happen to America. We were the smart ones. We cared about freedom and would do anything to protect it. Dad was proud of me and ultimately proud of himself for how he raised me. I was informed and ready. I was a freedom-loving, patriotic young man prepared for the worst.

The recent phenomenon of "prepping" isn't new to paranoid Americans. People have been doing it for decades, if not for over a century now. It's only in the past few decades it has become really popular. Mainstream big box stores like Costco sell items like a "1 Year Food Storage Kit" for $3,999.99.[1] It might sound like a lot of money, but this kit features 31,500 servings and they'll deliver it to your home in a pallet that is "black-wrapped for security and privacy." Walmart will sell you a "1-Year, 1-Person Emergency Food Storage Kit" for $1,305.81.[2] Prepping is big business in America now.

We were prepping, however, in a poor white-trashy way, which meant we had bullets, wild animals we could kill for food, and of course to kill commies. Dad didn't have the money to buy many proper prepping supplies. We had plenty of gun powder, lead and a lot of junk which could very well come in handy during an apocalypse. Our survival focus was based on firepower, living off the land and hiding in the hills which we knew better than anyone.

Along with my ambitions of killing commies for a living, I was taught how to prep for invasions. The movie *Red Dawn* was my reality and confirmation of what I was taught and what I knew to be true. It was also a fantasy and a nightmare at the same time. Dad would say all my friends and our relatives would probably die because they were busy playing sports or doing other stupid things. He said sports existed in America only to distract all of us from the realities that were taking place with the destruction of our country. Sports were a part of the Conspiracy.

Every day it seemed Dad would go on a rant about how something really bad was going to happen "real soon." I moved out thirty years ago and to this day, he still goes on about how something really bad is going to happen "real soon." How it was going to happen was always interesting. Would it be the Russians or Cubans invading us? It could be the communists in South America who would come in through Mexico. It could be all of the communists who were already here running the government. Dad didn't care how it was going to happen and he never told me how it was going to happen. He just said that in the next year or two, America would be radically different and our freedoms would all be mostly gone. I heard this first from dad in 1979. He repeated the same thing to me in 2015 - thirty-six years later.

Of course there were many ways that we would prepare for the worst, but there were also ways in which we could try to fight the inevitableness of enslavement.

"Support Your Local Police Force and Keep Them Independent" is a paranoid and racist program that the John Birch Society implemented in 1958 during the civil rights era. It's still a program today perpetuated by the Birch Society. One aspect of this program, (that's not focused on keeping black people down and out) is the fear that when the federal government determines that the time is right to take everyone hostage (think Hitler and his SS) using federal and state agencies (i.e. CIA, FBI, DEA, Homeland Security, Army, Marines, United Nation Peace Keepers, State Patrol and others.), our local police departments would be independent and hopefully fight back. Dad said this is why it was important to support our local police departments. This is also why it was important for local police departments to have semiautomatic machine guns like the feds.

We assumed that our local police force would eventually be eliminated, so we were constantly getting ready. Dad had dozens of guns on the property and was always trying to barter for more. If the commies came at night, we were ready. He kept a gun under his bed on the floor. He kept one under the mattress, under the bathroom sink, behind the bedroom door, two in the closet, one in the nightstand and one under his pillow. He was prepared when we went to bed, except that he wouldn't be able to do much anyway if something horrific ever did happen. Dad was a heavy drinker and liked to take prescription pain pills to fall asleep.

Dad hoarded reloading equipment so we could make fresh bullets. He had stockpiles of gun powder, and other munitions. We had cases of MRE's (U.S. Government-issued "Meals Ready to Eat"), water purification systems, hundreds of gallons of gasoline and diesel, generators and more. We had NBC (Nuclear, Biological & Chemical) gear. We had equipment and instructions for booby traps. We were ready and if anyone wanted to come up our driveway to take us, we were committed to be "better off dead than red," and I knew what to do.

I'm not really certain that we were prepping to survive a horrific event as much as we were preparing for a gun fight. I remember Dad glorifying this scenario and looking forward to the day when the shit would hit the fan and he would be able to fight back in some sort of a last-stand fantasy where we would fight to the death to protect our private property. Dad and I shared this fantasy and ultimately I think he really wanted to play it out with me.

Unlike during the time when we were preparing, the preppers today are not considered freaks. They're glorified, supported and catered to by big business and there are millions of them in America. Millions of Americans tune in weekly to *Doomsday Preppers* a huge cable television show - the largest in the history of the National Geographic Channel.[3]

To be prepared for an emergency is a good thing. But there's a huge difference between being prepared for a disaster as opposed to preparing for an apocalypse - which will likely never happen. It's something that many preppers are quite confident will happen one day and may even be hoping it does. At a certain point, I would hope that reason would kick in and these preppers would move on and actually live a little bit.

But that's rarely the case. If you've ever known a serious prepper or a complete sociopathic right-wing fanatic, you might understand. "He's armed everyone... including the kids... He drills them weekly. This is where things get real…. At best, he forces them to kill or maim at an age where they cannot remotely grasp the consequences of their actions. At worst, he turns them into threats needing neutralization. I understand that Dr. Perez wants his family to prepare to defend themselves, but arming children for combat is child abuse." This was within a review in PJ Media of *Doomsday Preppers*, Episode 16 titled, "The Time of Reckoning" that aired in 2012.[4]

Like anything, the paranoia of prepping can be carried too far. Not only because of the amount of stockpiling going on, but rather by how fear and paranoia can affect one's personality, mindset, character and ultimately the quality of life one can enjoy (and allow others and their children to enjoy too). Those who get lost in the world of prepping lose out on living life in the present and preparing for the real future. Living in paranoia makes it all that much easier for these people to entertain increasingly far-out conspiracy theories (like being rounded up and put into FEMA concentration camps or being disarmed by Obama's secret police). In the end, prepping is all based on paranoia and fear.

Dad was never really good at fixing things or making them work right. He was awesome at collecting and hoarding junk that he hoped one day would end up being very valuable in a bizarre Mad Max-like apocalyptic nightmare. With all his junk, he hoped he would either be able to assemble some sort of vehicle that would be good in a world like that or he'd be able to barter with his junk. Dad's junk also brought in a little money as occasionally someone would be in need of a part off some car and he would oftentimes have it.

Regardless of the backwoods junkyard that I grew up with, we were armed, prepped and seriously informed about the threats all around us. The impending overthrow, collapse of our own government or even better, an invasion of foreign troops, as in *Red Dawn*, was imminent.

Of course, nothing has ever happened and all the ammo, guns, expired cases of stolen MRE's and the tons and tons of rusty cars, trucks, boats and junk are all still sitting there to this day.

I can't comprehend the utter disappointment that must frustrate and literally make Dad go insane knowing that one day the shit is definitely for sure going to hit the fan, but it still hasn't. It has to be incredibly crushing to know that tomorrow could be the day - but it never is.

Being raised to be a prepper meant that I was taught to be selfish. I was taught that we were smarter than our neighbors and our friends.

We had no empathy for others. If they weren't prepping, that was their fault. Not ours. We were reclusive, paranoid and narcissistic.

Not only were we armed against UN Storm Troopers, we were armed against our neighbors - our fellow American citizens. We didn't care. It was going to be a dog-eat-dog world and when the shit did hit the fan, if they needed our help - too bad. Had our neighbors or other family members listened to our warnings, they too would have been prepared like us, so they were on their own.

For all we knew, people made fun of us. Looking back, I'd have to guess that most people thought Dad and I were at least a little crazy. And while there have been no real studies or research yet on the subject of the relationship between prepping and mental illness; I can't imagine that there will ever be an honest conclusion because the belief system of the prepper is built upon fear, narcissism and hostility towards reason.

Because preppers are heavy into conspiracy theories, their intense and irrational fear can not only be completely nuts, but deadly as well. This anxiety and uncertainness leads to craziness and eventually can lead to murder or domestic terrorism.

Nancy Lanza, the single mother of Sandy Hook killer Adam Lanza who slaughtered twenty children and seven adults was a huge fan of *Doomsday Preppers*. She was also a gun-hoarding survivalist and was preparing for an economic disaster in America. She taught Adam about guns, prepping and violence. Adam had some documented mental issues and a mother who herself clearly had some mental and emotional shortcomings.[5]

Adam's mom was a lot like my dad. Adam was trained to use weapons and at some point, lacking empathy, broke down and put four bullets into his mother before committing a tragic massacre.[6] Perhaps

Adam's mom should have been more prepared for reality. I think his mother is ultimately responsible for the murders of those twenty-seven Americans. Perhaps Adam's father should have worked harder for custody of his mentally ill son rather than leaving him to be raised by his weirdo ex-wife. She was the inspiration who taught her son how to be a domestic terrorist.

When unfit paranoid parents raise their children in their own image, bad things can happen - especially when empathy and rational thought are not involved.

Timothy McVeigh and Terry Nichols were avid preppers who were also responsible for the killing of 168 people and injuring over 600 at the Oklahoma City Bombing in 1995.[7]

The Olympic Park bomber, Eric Rudolph, was heavily into prepping and hid from authorities for nearly five years in the woods before he was caught. He was only able to do that because of his survival skills.[8]

In 2012, Washington state survivalist Peter Keller shot and killed his wife and daughter so he wouldn't have to worry about them anymore. He then locked himself in a bunker he made in a state park where he eventually killed himself after a standoff with local police. Keller couldn't wait any longer for the world to end - so he ended it on his own.[9]

The Branch Davidians in the Waco Siege possessed hundreds of guns and stockpiled tons of ammo and survival equipment. Weapon violations and their reluctance to communicate with federal agents led to the horrific event where a total of eighty six people died. Many were children. The Branch Davidians believed in the apocalypse and started their own.[10]

The Ruby Ridge Incident happened in large part ultimately because of Randy Weaver's extreme prepping which was fueled by his association with the Aryan Nations and his wife's belief that the apocalypse was imminent. Three people died at Ruby Ridge.[11] All of these events and many others have convinced many Americans that our government is determined to take away their freedoms and guns.

Every militia organization in America is prepping today. Every white nationalist group in America is prepping. A lot of normal-appearing people are prepping. All of these extreme right-wing organizations and their members have deep-rooted beliefs fueled by paranoia with hints of white supremacy from the Ku Klux Klan and conspiracy theories from the John Birch Society. As American preppers continue to breed and raise their children in a culture of fear and paranoia, we can expect more acts of domestic terrorism to haunt our daily news.

Preppers and their paranoia are really no different from America's "Military-Industrial Complex" problem. Our government and military, it seems, are always involved in a conflict on this planet somewhere in hopes of "spreading democracy and ending tyranny in our world".[12]

Even though the cold war ended decades ago, many Americans believe that it never ended. Many believe that the Soviets never got rid of any of their nukes and are actively rebuilding to destroy America.[13]

"Russia presents the greatest threat to our national security," General Joseph Dunford said to the Senate Armed Services committee on Thursday, July 9th, 2015 during his confirmation hearing to be the next Chairman of the Joints Chief of Staff.[14]

President Eisenhower warned us all in his Farewell Radio and Television Address to the American people on January 18th, 1961, "down the long lane of the history yet to be written, America knows that this world of ours, ever growing smaller, must avoid becoming a community of dreadful fear and hate, and be, instead, a proud confederation of mutual trust and respect." He added, "Disarmament, with mutual honor and confidence, is a continuing imperative. Together we must learn how to compose differences, not with arms, but with intellect and decent purpose."[15]

Robert Welch called "Eisenhower a conscious, dedicated agent of the communist conspiracy" shortly after this speech and perhaps because of another line within it: "steady progress toward our ultimate goal has been made."[16][17] That line signified that progress was being made in the reduction of nuclear arms between the two super powers. What it meant to me was that we were being tricked by the Russians to reduce our stockpile, all the while knowing that they would not reduce theirs. We believed Americans were being tricked and Eisenhower was a traitor.

Presumably, all preppers are likely to be seriously depressed and completely frustrated. It seems like every year or so, some Mayan or someone else says the world will end and then it doesn't. Dad was always saying stuff like this. When Bill Clinton got elected for a second term and survived an impeachment; Dad predicted a civil war in which the White House would burn down if Clinton was allowed to remain in power. It never happened.

During the Y2K panic - nothing happened. The horrors of 9/11 were just the beginning of the end of the world, then ISIS, then a black man gets elected twice and now all of us are threatened with a woman becoming president! All of these unreal scenarios feed the prepper lifestyle and for a lot of people, they are all signs that the end is near.

One of the Republican candidates who ran in the 2016 Presidential Race, Ben Carson, also believes that the end is near. At one point he was a front runner for the candidacy. "He fully embraces an apocalyptic vision of the American nightmare that is upon us. More than anyone else (in the Republican field of candidates), he represents a particular fringe fraction of the conservative movement," wrote Paul Waldman in article in *The Week* titled, "Ben Carson is ready for the coming American apocalypse."[18]

In the same article, "Carson has also suggested (during an interview on Fox News earlier in 2015) that there might not be an election at all in 2016, because by then Barack Obama would have sent America spiraling downward into anarchy."

The rhetoric coming out of Ben Carson's mouth sounds no different to me than the paranoia and hate coming from Dad.

There's a good reason for this. Both of them are heavily influenced by the John Birch Society. In an interview in 2014 on Fox News with

Megan Kelly, Carson stated, "This guy wrote a book in 1958 called *The Naked Communist* and it laid out their whole agenda. You would think by reading it that it was written last year. Showing what they are trying to do, to American families, to our Judeo-Christian faith, our morality."[19] Carson never elaborated or was asked who "they" are although I'm quite certain that he was referring to the commies that Dad always talked about.

The Naked Communist was written by W. Cleon Skousen, an avid supporter of the John Birch Society. Skousen wrote other things for the John Birch Society as well including a lengthy pamphlet titled, *The Communist Attack on the John Birch Society.*[20]

I was never scared that preppers, or someone like Dad, or even the John Birch Society or KKK would be a threat to America. Mostly, I was just irritated and sad that my Dad was a nut job who spent so much time "training" me, and then didn't want anything to do with me from the point at which he no longer controlled my life.

These days, I can't watch the news without hearing the same propaganda that was force-fed to me when I was a teenager. I'm confident that there will continue to be more Waco and Sandy Hook incidents, and probably even more horrifying mass-murders inspired by extreme right-wing paranoia and hate. I wonder at what point these militia organizations and hate groups are going to launch a coordinated offensive against the White House, a state capital building, a local city hall or a police department?

The millionaire ranch farmer in Clark County, Nevada, Cliven Bundy, in April 2014 was a little blip on the screen, (that didn't work out) when he fought the government over unpaid grazing fees. Over a thousand right-wing nut jobs with sniper rifles and machine guns were ready to pull their triggers at the Bundy standoff. How many of those guys with their machine guns were disappointed that no one got killed? [21]

I would, with certainly, tell you nearly all of them were seriously bummed out that federal agents displayed patience and professionalism in resolving this one dispute. The irony about all of these extremist right-wing paranoids preparing for some catastrophic event to happen is that they will likely be the ones to take the first shots. Probably to "wake us all up" Dad would say. Maybe then Dad can validate his otherwise pointless existence with an "I told you so."

9 IT'S ONLY ROCK & ROLL, BUT I LIKE IT

My junior year in high school was a significant turning point in my life. Puberty had kicked in. Music, cars and girls were more important than following in Dad's paranoid lifestyle. I still had my ninja stars and collection of survival gear, but I was more into normal American teenager activities like hanging out with my friends.

The real life changer for me, however, was that I was becoming popular in high school. I also had a girlfriend and I was playing bass guitar in the high school band. Being the bass player came about after the former bass player graduated and the band (which meant pep band, stage band and concert band) needed someone to take over playing the bass. The only problem with this was that I wasn't into arts and didn't know how to play a bass guitar. I could set traps to catch critters, build a hidden bunker in the woods and stack firewood properly, but I didn't have a clue about how to play the bass.

One of my good friends in the same grade played the guitar in band and said it would be cool if I learned how to play and joined the band. The high school band teacher agreed and let me take home a school-owned, bass guitar over the summer before my junior year.

"Wipe Out," by the Surfaris was the first song I ever learned to play and I figured it out myself by learning how to read sheet music.

I'd practice all the time at home over the summer and Mom and Dad were skeptically supportive. It was an electric bass and I didn't have an amp so it was quiet and I didn't bother anyone at home. I still helped Dad with chores every day, but I now had a car and a job at McDonalds. My siblings were old enough to help with chores around the house and property.

Playing bass in high school band was very cool. It exposed me to a new level of popularity, normalcy and brought social privileges that being a right-wing paranoid teenager might not expect to attain.

Being socially-accepted by friends and teachers was a huge confidence booster that inched me towards being a normal kid. In addition, I was class president now and very involved with school activities.

My junior and senior years were somewhat normal or at least more normal than previous years. My grades were much better. I went to parties. I was in FBLA (Future Business Leaders of America) and the Debate Club at the high school. The guitar player and I were disc jockeys at the high school dances after home football games. I was doing things like performing in lip sync contests and was even in a high school play. I played "Francis" - a 14 year-old boy pretending to be a girl so his parents could inherit a lot of money from the boy's grandma who hated little boys. I was cross dressing in a high school production! Mom and Dad didn't see the play.

I wasn't really embarrassed by how I behaved in my earlier years at the high school or even back in junior high. I didn't possess the mental aptitude to understand how narcissistic, pathetic and wrong I was. Looking back, I don't think my classmates judged me by how extreme I was or how extreme my parents were either.

The biggest change for me during these years was the influence of an adult looking out for me and my best interests. My high school band teacher was a friend, a mentor and an inspiration. He was without a doubt, the first real father figure in my life who really cared about what was best for me and my future. To this day, he's had a positive influence on my life and I cannot thank him enough. Dad hated him and called him a hippy - because his hair was a little bit long and it sat comfortably on his shoulders.

My band teacher (after I graduated from high school, I called him Chuck as we were on a first name basis) talked to me like I was a real person. He treated me with respect and gave me plenty of encouragement. He was a free-thinker and a super nice, cool guy (and still is). Overall, he was the most popular teacher at the high school. Everybody liked him. I got to be close to him. I took every band class I could (three my senior year) mostly to be in his class and because I really enjoyed playing music. He was also the drama teacher and was the reason why I was participating in a high school play.

When I told Chuck during my senior year I wanted to play bass for a living and be a rock star, he said that was fine, but, I needed a back-up plan and should go to college so I could have a good job one day if the rock star plan didn't work out. Our senior class had a time capsule in which everyone wrote down their dream for the future. My dream was to be on the cover of *Rolling Stone.*

During this time, school was a lot of fun and I spent a lot of time there. I felt normal and wanted. I had friends who wanted to hang out with me. I felt like I belonged. My parents hated this. They complained that I wasn't at home enough.

I would often report back to them about how well school was going with my grades and various achievements. For some reason, they hated this. They would both often call me "Mr. Wonderful," in a condescending tone. Whenever I presented my achievements and the joy I was experiencing in hopes of gaining approval, Mom and Dad were resentful about my new outgoingness. They created an environment of mockery. They ridiculed me in front of my brother and sisters about how "great" I was. "Well aren't you special," they'd both say. I'd tell them I got an A on a test and they'd both put me down. "You're Number One,"

Dad would say in his sarcastic manner. Over time I quit sharing as much, yet, for some reason, I still shared plenty with them - hoping to make them proud of me.

I hated their attitudes and didn't understand why they were so cruel. Dad was seriously irritated (and jealous I'm certain) by my new persona and would be extremely irritable when I would do something that bothered him. If I chewed food or gum with my mouth open, he'd slap the top of my head with his hand and tell me to "knock it off." If I bit into a carrot or a potato chip or something that would make noise, he'd cringe at the sound (his eyes would twitch) and he would slap me on my head. If I was across the room, he'd tell me to be quiet. Dad wasn't happy.

In a lot of respects, this new disconnect with my parents also created a major disconnect between my siblings and me. All of us, with the example set forth by our parents, embraced an animosity that has never gone away. I think they resented my overachieving ways and treated me like there was something wrong with me.

It's very frustrating that my brother and sisters and I aren't close. I wish we were. Even though we all grew up together in the same musty double-wide trailer, all of us had very different childhood experiences and relationships with our parents. None of them had the same type of relationship I had with my Dad. The one bond or similarity that we all share, however, is that none of us got along with each other, nor are any of us close to this day. Sadly, this was because of the hostile atmosphere that existed in our childhoods created by Mom and Dad. They failed to promote love or compassion in us for each other.

Oddly enough, Dad hardly ever propagated the conspiracies of the John Birch Society to my brother or sisters, except he once sent my youngest sister to Birch Camp when she was fifteen. Both parents did push their racism and bigotry on all of us, but left my siblings out of the brainwashing and fear mongering that I had endured. He once explained this by telling me I had the "intellectual fortitude" to comprehend the inner-workings and complexities of the Conspiracy and they didn't.

My siblings lived in a different world and with a different father than the one I knew. The focus and expectations in their lives were not the same as my father had for me. To this day they seem to have no concept of what I lived through. As a result, we have little in common and quite different views of our father.

What was still inside my mind, though, was this image of our perfect American family in our perfect American home. This was the portrayal of our family by Mom and Dad. They constantly spoke about how great our family was and how our home was just wonderful. To reinforce this notion, they spoke poorly about everyone else we knew including their kids, their jobs, their beliefs, and their houses. Whether it was an aunt, our uncles, a grandma or cousins and friends, there was always something negative and condescending to be said about everyone else. My parents were constantly critical of everyone outside of our family.

Being rather popular and outgoing in high school and having fun with friends meant that I was failing Dad's wishes. Ultimately, he asserted that I was assisting the Communist Conspiracy by not doing everything I could. I still did a few things with him involving the John Birch Society and firewood, but the survivalist fantasies and mercenary dreams were old news. I tried to distance myself from being cynical and paranoid. Not to mention, there were things I'd hear or see that always seemed to contradict the brainwashing that came from Dad and the John Birch Society.

Despite that, I would still appease him with an interest in Birch Society literature and videos, and would act like I was interested and understood the things he'd say.

When we'd sit down to have dinner at the dining table, he would place a new *American Opinion Newsletter* next to my plate. I'd say "thanks" and skim it while eating. To avoid conflict, I would play along by going to Birch Society meetings, but I certainly wasn't into it anymore. It wasn't because I wasn't buying their message, as much as that I didn't really care anymore.

To an outsider driving up our driveway, we must have looked like a bunch of hillbillies living in the middle of a junkyard. As I said before, Dad was a hoarder of junk. By my senior year, there were well over forty vehicles on our property (spread out over four or more acres in the woods). There were also numerous pigs, chickens and goats running around or tied up to trees. Dad had a few wood sheds and all kinds of other storage containers. I thought nothing of our lifestyle until my friends came to my house and asked me one day,

"What's your dad doing with all this junk?" I said "he's fixing stuff up and making cool things." They looked at me like I was crazy.

That was the first time that I was really embarrassed about how I lived. No one had ever said anything to my parents regarding all of Dad's junk. I eventually started to complain a little bit, but Mom made excuses for him by saying that he was working on it. We were white trash and I was now realizing this and no longer felt like I fit in at home. Dad of course never fixed anything.

Even though I was making internal changes on the person my mother and father raised, I was still not thinking about going to college. The paranoia I possessed dictated that I still somewhat believed that getting "educated" would be dangerous. Despite that fear, I felt like I could handle it without turning into a liberal. Going to college was important because I wanted a career where I didn't have to grow up and live like a hillbilly. More importantly, however, I didn't want to upset my parents by telling them I wanted to go to college. Rather, at Dad's persistence, I enlisted in the Washington Army National Guard during high school and began my six-year commitment in March 1986 before graduating high school a few months later.

At my high school graduation party, I was lucky enough to win a donated trip to Maui for two that included airfare and a condo. I took one of my best friends named Rick. We had an agreement that if he won, he'd take me and if I won, I'd take him. I also invited Chuck the band teacher to go with us. To my surprise and delight, he did. It was a fantastic trip and one of the best times that I've ever had in my life. Those last two years of high school helped me dramatically.

If it wasn't for being the bass player in the high school band, I can't imagine who or what I'd be today. The path that Dad and Mom had set forth for me was a complete path of destruction, extreme paranoia and misery. Music and my high school band teacher, Chuck, most likely saved me from being just like my dad.

10 THE EFFECTS OF TEACHING YOUR CHILD TO BE A PARANOID

"All my life I tried to find a way, all my life I tried.
All my life I tried to get away, all my life I died."

These are the lyrics in the chorus to one of the first songs I ever wrote. The song was called "Memory" and was performed many times by an alternative rock band I was in during the early nineties in the Seattle area. I was the lead singer and bass player.

We played at a club in Tacoma one night and my younger sister (not the youngest) was there watching us for the first time. We played "Memory" and after the show the band and I were all sitting in a booth with my sister and some other people.

Out of the blue she says to me "that one song was about Dad wasn't it?"

I was blown away when she asked that. I said "It was. How did you know?"

She said she could tell by the words.

It wasn't until that night that I realized from the age of seventeen, I had been desperately trying not to be anything like my dad.

I had previously never thought that I had issues with my childhood or parents. I never spent any time examining my childhood as problematic. Looking back, however, I realized my childhood was full of delusions about life, love, people and the events that made and shaped the world.

Regardless of the life that I was living now on my own, I struggled with paranoia, depression and low self-esteem. I did a pretty good job of acting like a normal person, but sometimes I'd fall into despair.

"Since August 1945, the Communists have, on average, taking over seven thousand newly enslaved subjects every hour. And please remember that these people, whether in Indonesia or Iraq or Korea, have the same love for their families. Think of concentration camps with the same despairing horror, and feel the same pain under torture, as do you and I," said Robert Welch in his *Blue Book*.

This stuff was pounded into my skull when I was a young teenager. This was the truth that my "loving Christian parents" wanted me to embrace. My mind was dedicated to fear and my outlook on life was bleak, supported by fatalistic propaganda from the John Birch Society. I never thought that I'd live long enough to see twenty or beyond.

Dad's thoughts had no real basis in reality. He was unable to process or handle criticism or challenges to his thought processes. He was an ignorant man who believed that he was smarter than everyone else. He was my mentor, hero and teacher. He taught me to be like him.

Mom provided some motherly comfort, but didn't dare infringe upon Dad's methods with me as she never wanted to upset him.

Dad taught me that if someone challenged your statements or beliefs, they did so because they were scared or intimidated and couldn't handle the truth. He said that all liberals were brainwashed and trained to ignore the truths regarding America. Sometimes they would fail to comprehend the situation or reality, so they'd make fun of the messenger with ridicule and contempt. They would use "learned" tactics, Dad would say, on how to avoid finding out the real truth from a good conservative American. Arguing with a liberal was a complete waste of time, he'd say. They were too dumb, too brainwashed and there was no way that we could change their minds.

"Liberals always change the subject and that's how they deal with reality," Dad said. It was an organized deflection of reality.

The Conspiracy needed liberals as they were pawns in the New World Order. Liberals focused on issues of animal rights, environmental rights and education instead of dealing with the ultimate crisis facing America - communism and the elimination of the insiders running the conspiracy.

Every time someone argued with me about anything, I felt contempt. I felt ridiculed. I felt like they were telling me I was stupid and wrong. Just having someone argue with me or having my point of view questioned made me angry. It's staggering and sad how many friends and family members won't talk to me anymore because of how I used to argue with them and even belittled them. Being an extreme right-wing know-it-all can make you behave like an ass and make it so you don't have very many real friends.

Sadly, being raised by a paranoid right-wing kook can definitely hamper your ability to live life without being a bit paranoid yourself. I thought I knew everything, but the reality was that I was clearly ignorant of many things. My ignorance has been anything but bliss. Constantly seeking knowledge, trying to be self-aware, empathetic and honest have helped me.

If Google had been around in the eighties, life would have been so much easier. Before the internet became dominant in our methods of receiving news and information, Dad's propaganda and the words of the John Birch Society were my only real source of information. We rejected everything else that we read or saw on the news. I was taught not to believe anything the media presented.

I was now living on my own in the late eighties. I was a soldier in the Washington Army National Guard and enrolled in a local community college working towards a degree in Parks and Recreation. This career selection ensured that there would be little chance of a good liberal brainwashing because of the subject matter needed to get that type of degree. Dad was okay with this career selection of mine even though he still worried that going to college was a bad decision. I was also working as a landscaper and spent a lot of evenings either practicing or playing gigs with my band.

Before I began college, Dad and I had a conversation discussing what it meant to be "open-minded." He said people who had open minds refused simple truths and needed to cloud those truths with details that weren't relevant or important. "If your mind was open," Dad would say, "it meant that you were able to be brainwashed and accept a liberal or alternative point of view." Having an open-mind meant that you weren't mentally strong and capable of handling the cold hard truth. This conversation was important to Dad as it was a reminder to me to make sure that I didn't get brainwashed by my commie college professors.

During this time, which was about a year and a half after graduating from high school, Dad had ramped up his efforts with managing my information and education. He constantly invited me to various John Birch Society Speaking Bureau events and sometimes I would go. He would send me copies of various Birch Society publications in the mail and would later ask me questions about the stories inside.

When I would go back and visit my parents, he would give me extra copies of *The New American* and tell me to take the magazines and distribute them. When Dad had a doctor or dentist appointment, he would take in a copy of *The New American* or an older *American Opinion Magazine* and leave one with the stacks of *People* and *Popular Science* magazines littering the waiting rooms. When I was younger and had a dentist appointment, he would always give me a magazine to leave inside the waiting room, and I would. Dad asked me to leave copies of Birch Society magazines in various places around the college campus. He was spreading the truth through my efforts.

Almost everything I was ever taught by Dad has now been questioned and cross-examined by me. It used to be a constant struggle to break free from the paranoia and fears that were inside my head.

When I saw a plane or a helicopter in the sky over my parents' property while growing up, I was suspicious. I knew, "They're spying on us." I'd even go so far as to stand near the trunk of a tree so they didn't see me if I couldn't find cover. Dad taught me this and he even covered up certain items on the property with outdoor camo net that he stole from Fort Lewis so they couldn't be seen from the air.

"When they use the word 'freedom,' they don't mean freedom like our forefathers meant," Dad would say. *The Encyclopedia of Marxism* explains that "Freedom is the right and capacity of people to determine their own actions, in a community which is able to provide for the full development of human potentiality." So in other words, freedom means communism. When I saw the word or heard the word freedom, I knew it was a trick.

Dad said the Communists sabotaged the word "peace" as well.

Fred Koch in his book, *A Business Man Looks at Communism*, said that "most communist fronts have the word PEACE in them. Everybody wants peace, of course, but to a Communist, the word peace means communism."

When John Lennon sang, "Give peace a chance," all I could imagine (no pun intended) was that the Beatles wanted me to be a communist slave. Dad hated the Beatles and still does. I grew up hating the Beatles as well. I didn't hate them because of their music of course, but because I had believed that they wanted my family and me to be communist slaves.

"When they use the peace sign (the V-sign hand gesture in which your index and middle finger are raised and parted like a V), it means communist victory," Dad said. I never did question him why both Nixon and Churchill often used the peace sign. Dad never said either of them were Communists. "Most people have no idea what they're doing when they say they want peace," Dad used to say. "They're playing into the enemy's hands."

I was taught that women, especially the unhappy ones "who were essentially worthless," were the ones in favor of equal rights. Dad said organizations such as NOW (National Organization for Women) didn't exist solely for women's rights nearly as much as they were for taking away our rights as American men. "Women's Liberation is definitely planned by Communists... To break down American families and morality," said Robert Welch. "Most women have too much sense to want careers, preferring instead to do what nature intended them to do."[1]

I have no memories whatsoever of Dad embracing or kissing my mother. I can't even recall them ever hugging. I can't even imagine them embracing with my eyes closed. Dad always talked down to her and treated her without respect.

Mom wasn't in favor of Women's Lib either of course.

Dad would never physically engage Mom in front of us. He was great at making verbal threats, calling her names and putting her down. Mom used his PTSD as an excuse for his poor behavior. Mom always said "don't upset your father. Just keep quiet. It's not worth it to upset him."

Because of what happened to Dad and his buddies in Vietnam, Mom has spent the majority of her life protecting him - serving as a buffer, a bed full of excuses and comfort for him. He never had to deal with his issues and problems, mostly because Mom kept as many sources of frustration away from him as possible. She ultimately kept him from dealing with his real issues of survivor's guilt and shame. Mom just wanted everyone to be "happy."

Millions of people and veterans in this country have PTSD, some worse than others. Most of them, however, don't use it as an excuse to teach their kid to be a liar, a thief, a hypocrite, a sociopath, a racist, a sexist and a complete asshole.

Mom tried to leave Dad in the early nineties. I was in between classes at college one day when she called crying and said she really needed to talk to me right away. I drove out to their house (over an hour away) and she confided to me that she was going to leave Dad.

She said that she couldn't take it anymore and that he was a terrible person and she deserved to be happy.

I was so happy for her and so proud that she had finally decided to leave the hate, paranoia and fear that was a constant in her home. I told her that I was proud of her and completely understood her motivations for leaving. "Dad's an asshole and you deserve better. If I could divorce him from being my dad, I would" I said to her, trying to give her assurances that she wasn't completely alone.

Days had passed and Mom still hadn't said anything to Dad. She still hadn't left either. In a matter of a few weeks, they had talked and Dad convinced her that his PTSD made him the way he was and if she stayed, he would get help. Mom stayed put and anytime there was a conflict with Dad, Mom would resolve the issue by still insisting his PTSD was the reason he was the way he was and there was nothing that could be done about it. Mom gave me a copy of a book about PTSD, told me to read it, and explained that I shouldn't get hurt or angry when he was cruel or mean.

Dad went to a VA Hospital to get help with his PTSD and has been in regular therapy since the early nineties. Therapy has never helped Dad.

With the exception of a few Japanese and Hawaiian people where we lived, I didn't like people who weren't white. Dad claimed that black people, for the most part, were lazy, didn't want to work and bought drugs with their welfare checks. They hurt America. The good black people were called "African Americans" and the bad ones were "niggers," he'd say. Mexicans were called "wetbacks" and none of them were welcome in this country because they took jobs away from real Americans (white people) by working for less. Asians were taking over

America, he said, because after they entered our country, the government would give them each $50,000 so they could buy a 711, a gas station, or a similar business. Asian people had a lot of money that our own government ultimately gave away, according to Dad.

I used to believe that all homosexuals, atheists, immigrants, liberals and anything and anyone that wasn't like us, were all out to destroy me. When I heard the words humanist, environmentalist, feminist, educated or equal and civil rights, I'd be irritated, suspicious and angry. Those were all code words for communism.

Dad equated black people with Communists. He was so paranoid that he believed black people would take away his entitlements in this country. He hated black people because they wanted the same rights as white people. According to him, their desires for equal rights made them pawns of the Communist Conspiracy. I believed for years that Martin Luther King Jr. was training all black people to be Communists and Malcolm X and the Black Panthers were out to kill white people for sport.

Mom used to say if all the black men in America married only white women and had babies, then eventually there'd be no black people left and that would be a good thing. I don't think she meant to be racist as much as a banana really wants to be called fruit. If one of my sisters ever came home with a black man they knew that Dad would kill him, because he told them so.

I was initially confronted with my racism on the first day of Army Basic Training in Fort Dix, New Jersey in November, 1986. Every room in our barracks had four bunk beds. Six of those eight beds in my room were occupied by black guys. This was the first time I had really been around black people for more than just a few minutes. I was struggling, but in no time, all the grueling training was so overwhelming that being friendly and normal with them wasn't difficult. They were nice guys. These must have been the nice black people dad had told me about. My Drill Sergeants were also black.

Dad was constantly trying to dehumanize our enemies or anyone who didn't believe the things that he knew to be true.

People who lived in other countries outside of America were not really normal or civilized like us, he'd say. If they didn't dress like Americans or act and do the things we did, then they weren't exactly developed or advanced like us.

People who weren't American were subhuman. And because these other people were less human than I was, it was easy to hate them and be completely unaffected by their deaths. Stories of horrific war tactics - using suicide bombers, children and women, burning people inside of used tires - led me to believe that our enemies are inhuman and not worthy of humane treatment.

Hollywood helped this belief with the first real big zombie movie, *Night of the Living Dead*, which came out in 1968 and served as a metaphor for the impending communist invasion. The mantra kept repeating in my head: communists aren't human. They're zombies. That's why it's so easy to kill them. Zombies are commies...

There haven't been many studies yet regarding the effects of raising children far outside the parameters of what most would consider an ordinary childhood. There has been some exploration on some of the most recent American killers (Adam Lanza, the Aurora killer, the Columbine killers, Timothy McVeigh, and others.) which has led to no satisfactory conclusion on why young people commit such terrifying, horrible acts. Most parents of these killers were adamant that their child was loved very much and that there was no way they could have foreseen the atrocities committed. All of these parents were either shocked or killed by the actions of their killer child.

These parents in my opinion were ignorant to their own mistakes. Normal, well-balanced and loved kids don't commit these atrocities. These parents should have been aware that their children were disconnected from them and others. There was little if any real connection between any of these little monsters and their parents. Had there been mutual love or recognition, these killers might have chosen different paths. My constant desire for love and approval from my parents, I believe, kept me from being another sad statistic in the world of extreme American patriotism - often referred to as domestic terrorism.

Mom knew what Dad was pounding into my head. She knew that he was hateful, fearful and paranoid. She was afraid of him, but mostly, she was afraid of losing her "perfect American family" - something she had always wanted.

Dad raised me to be paranoid. He taught me to trust no one. He taught me bigotry, selfishness and entitlement. He taught me how to hate myself and others. He taught me how to blame and how to lie. He taught me fear. He taught me hypocrisy and showed me rage.

Mom taught me through her silence, that Dad's efforts with me met her approval. To this day, she insists I had a very normal American childhood and I should just "get over" whatever issues I may have.

What Dad ultimately taught me, however, was to prepare for the worst, because nothing good was ever coming our way. And if something good did happen, it probably wasn't real and we were being tricked into believing it was. What this led to was my constant fear and paranoia that happiness isn't genuine, real or deserved, while misery, fear and contempt are normal and accepted.

When I was twenty, Dad got me a 9 mm semi-automatic pistol. It was a stainless steel Taurus PT92 complete with a 17 round clip. The gun was beautiful and I kept it real clean. It felt good. I felt empowered when I held it. My thinking was, "Nobody should mess with me."

One evening in late 1989, I was driving around in the Hilltop Neighborhood of Tacoma with my shiny gun sitting in the passenger seat of my Ford Bronco II. I wasn't going anywhere in particular. I was just driving around and I was angry. The gun was loaded and the safety was off.

The Hilltop neighborhood back then was rough. It was littered with gangs. The Crips and Bloods had migrated up from California and had established themselves in Tacoma. In September 1989 there was a horrific shootout between a bunch of gang bangers and some Army Rangers from Fort Lewis at a party on the Hilltop. They called it the Ash Street Shootout. Hundreds of bullets were fired. [2]

The shootout happened essentially because a white Army Ranger who lived on the hilltop was tired of all the gang and drug activity. He had put up video cameras to provide surveillance of the area to try to help stop their activities. The gang members were angry. Late one night after some verbal exchanges, they drove by the party and started shooting at the Army Rangers. Of course, the Rangers fired back.

It was horrible and all over the national news. US Army Rangers were being shot at by black gang bangers and I was angry. That wasn't right. I wanted to help.

With everything I was ever taught by Dad, having a gun enabled my rage and fueled my paranoia. I could have done something right then and there to make America a "better place." A gun in my possession with the extreme right-wing brainwashing I received as a teenager only made matters worse. I never pointed it at anyone that night.

I'm confident that if I had found myself threatened or in a confrontation with a gang member, I would have taken action. I drove by plenty of black people that night who were standing on street corners, walking down sidewalks and going into their homes. It was a surreal and ugly night that could have destroyed my life and the lives of others. After driving around for about an hour, I left the hilltop area, scared. I'm not sure if I was more afraid of what I might have done or that someone else might have shot back at me.

With everything going on inside my head, having a gun in my possession was a terrible mistake. A few days later I returned the gun to Dad and said I didn't need it. He wasn't happy. I never did tell him about my Hilltop story.

11 BRAVE MAN'S DEATH

In the summer of 1991, my Army National Guard unit based out of Fort Lewis, WA alerted me that I was in the process of being activated to full-time status because of the Gulf War. Everyone in my unit was placed on "alert status" meaning that we couldn't be more than seventy-five miles away from Fort Lewis at any given time. It seemed it would only be a matter of weeks or months before I'd get a call telling me to report for full-time duty and prepare to be sent to fight the war in the Middle East.

Over 200,000 American weekend warriors had to leave their fulltime jobs and families to go fight in the Gulf War.[1]

My military occupation specialty (MOS) in the National Guard was 68J, also known as an Aircraft Fire Control Repairman. I worked on the weapons and some of the related electronic systems on Cobra Helicopters for the 116th Attack Helicopter Troop. I was also still in community college, working a job and playing in a rock band during this time.

Prior to being placed on alert status, I had thrived and enjoyed my time in the National Guard. Every year for two weeks in the summer our unit, along with many other regional National Guard units, would go play "war" at the Yakima Firing Range.

This short stint was a lot of fun with poker games at night along with plenty of beer drinking. Once or twice a week, we'd all go fishing or float down the Yakima River on inner tubes for the day.

In just two years after enlisting in the National Guard I had been promoted to E-5 or a sergeant ranking. I took my role in the Guard seriously and was excelling in my skill set and knowledge of the weapon and electronic systems on the Cobra Helicopters.

In the summer "war" of 1990, I was so gung-ho in my performance out in the field that I was officially recognized by a three-star general. I was the only soldier in my unit to be awarded the Army Achievement Award in front of my peers in the middle of this "war." The general asked me if there was anything he could do for me. I told him I wanted to ride in the front gunner seat of a fully loaded Cobra while the pilot behind me fired all the rockets and unloaded the 20MM cannon. A couple of hours later I was up in the sky with rockets whizzing just inches away from my head as they destroyed an old rusty steel container used as a target. This was an awesome experience!

Dad was super proud of me and I was happy. The rush I received during this time was unlike anything I had experienced in my John Birch Society summer camp days. The need to excel and be recognized for my achievements was even stronger in me as a young adult.

When I received the call from my unit about being activated though, I was shocked and disappointed. I couldn't believe that not only was our country invading and protecting Kuwait to stop Saddam Hussein and his Red Army's advance, but that my part-time, weekend warrior National Guard unit was going to be sent to the Middle East to fight in a real war and likely all die for George Bush's "New World Order."

I was an exceptional part-time soldier and knew the Constitution better than most. I swore to defend it with my life, but this was ridiculous. Full-time soldiers train full-time for war. We trained one weekend a month and then played war for two weeks every summer. We weren't ready for this.

I was very distraught about the situation and called Dad to talk about how I felt about being placed on alert status and the war. Dad said that this war was necessary because Kuwait was loyal and a pro-American country that needed our support. I knew very little about Kuwait prior to this war other than it was a small country in the Middle East.

I was totally surprised that Dad believed America's presence and role in Kuwait was necessary and that he wasn't worried about me being sent to the Middle East. "You're an REMF (Rear End Mother F#@ker)! You'll be fine." he said. (REMF is a degrading term that infantrymen use to describe soldiers who possess technical skills and are not on the front lines in war. Because I worked on weapon systems, I did most of my work on a flight pad or in an aircraft hangar.) I was confused and upset after my conversation with Dad.

Not only was I fearful of going to war and likely fighting alongside UN Stormtroopers, I was also watching my fears of a New World Order coming to fruition. Dad didn't even seem concerned.

In President George Bush's (the elder) "Address before a Joint Session of the Congress on the Persian Gulf Crisis and the Federal Budget Deficit" on September 11, 1990, he let the entire world know that the New World Order was coming. "We stand today at a unique and extraordinary movement... Out of these troubled times...a new world order - can emerge: a new era - freer from the threat of terror, stronger in the pursuit of justice, and more secure in the quest for peace... This is the vision that I shared with President Gorbachev in Helsinki." [2]

This was the New World Order that I was warned about and now I might become a part of ushering it in. Further, Bush was working hand-in-hand with the Russian President on making this New World Order a reality!

I questioned Dad about why he thought this war was a good idea and even challenged his opinions, telling him that this was part of the New World Order he was normally against. He kept saying that the people in Kuwait needed our support and that this was a war worth fighting. If we didn't stop Hussein, he would probably take over the entire Middle East where we had lots of allies, he shared. I reminded him that Saddam Hussein was an anti-communist dictator whom we (the U.S.) supported in the eighties against Iran.[3] "This doesn't make any sense," I said. Dad said I was overreacting and military action was necessary. He refused to consider my arguments. At one point he said, "You probably won't have to go, but if you do, there's nothing you can do about it anyway."

Robert Welch and the John Birch Society were adamant about getting America out of the Vietnam War and had never really behaved as a "pro-war" organization.[4] I couldn't figure out why Dad was taking this position. My confusion continued to escalate. All I could imagine was either dying or fighting alongside UN troops. I would be playing a part in creating George Bush's New World Order.

Because of my depression about what was going on with the war and my National Guard unit, I quit going to my college classes. I had a hard time focusing on anything while on alert status. All I could think about was this unjustifiable war and how I didn't want to die for such a ridiculous cause. I didn't return my books or notify the school. I just quit going and never did return.

One day in the winter of 1991, I was in downtown Seattle. I don't remember why I was there, but I was alone and walking around. Somehow, I ended up at an antiwar rally at the steps of the King County Courthouse listening to protestors speak against the Gulf War. The speakers were saying how wrong this war was and how diplomacy and embargoes should be enforced to resolve the dispute. Many spoke out against imperialism. Not really a fan of public speaking, I somehow got the nerve up to walk toward the microphone. I grabbed it like I had something to say.

I told them my name and that I was in the Washington Army National Guard. "I just got placed on alert status and I'm probably going to have go fight in this Gulf War and I don't want to" I said. I commented that the war had nothing to do with our freedoms or the Constitution. "I think this war is stupid" was my concluding remark.

I felt great after speaking. They all clapped and the guy that grabbed the microphone from me thanked me for my service and honesty. I didn't feel alone even though I was likely surrounded by a bunch of liberals, hippies and socialists. I was proud of myself that day.

When I enlisted in the Army National Guard, I signed an oath pledging my allegiance to the Constitution and my life to defend it if necessary. There was nothing about defending the Constitution or America when we went to Kuwait and later Iraq. I didn't sign up to go kick some foreign ass for fun or adventure. I joined the military because I had a patriotic duty to do so and also, of course, because Dad convinced me that I should. But the thought of our leaders putting me in a deadly situation when there was no threat to our nation's sovereignty, in my mind, was betrayal.

I'm pretty sure that speaking at an anti-war rally was one the most liberal acts that I had committed in my life up until then, other than to enroll in a community college. Of course Dad never heard about it.

My unit stayed on active status, but was never actually sent to the Gulf War. A few months later, my time in the National Guard was over as my six-year commitment ended. I turned down the reenlistment bonus offered to me and ended my dream of becoming a pilot flying Apache Helicopters. I feared being shot down and killed by some Iraqis who weren't out to destroy America or our Constitution.

I never could confirm why Dad supported this war and he never offered to explain his position. Perhaps it was because the people he categorically hated (liberals and hippies) were so strongly against it, and this was enough to inspire his support. He had trained me to be prepared for war, but not this one. He wanted me to participate in it, though, even if it killed me.

12 LIVING THE DREAM

During my early twenties, I was enjoying a more carefree and fun lifestyle. Dad wasn't exactly thrilled with this and was confrontational about everything I was doing. He wanted to know who my friends were, when was I going to get a haircut, why I wasn't going to Birch Society meetings anymore, had I read the latest *The New American* and so on.

He'd often try to engage me regarding certain politicians or current domestic events like what had happened in Ruby Ridge and Waco. I did my best to ignore him or change the subject whenever these conversations came up. These catastrophic events and others outraged me, but I was able to suppress those feelings around Dad.

It was irritating and frustrating trying to get out of Dad's grasp. I did my best to stay away, and my communication with both Mom and Dad was on the decline. Even though I wasn't hanging around my siblings or parents much, it seemed that Dad was aware of everything I was doing.

"Are you a switch hitter?" he asked me on the phone one day.

"What?" I said.

"I heard that you like going to gay clubs in Seattle with your 'friend' Michael," he stated sarcastically.

I laughed. "Are you asking me if I'm gay Dad?" He didn't answer and I said, "No, I'm not gay Dad. But what if I was?"

He didn't respond to that either.

The conversation digressed as conversations with Dad always did when he wasn't in control. He didn't know my friend Michael was black, either.

I never shared with Dad that Michael and I went to this gay club all the time because there were plenty of straight single girls who went there to dance without worrying about being hit on by guys. It wasn't a hassle turning down the gay boys, and you could tell who the straight or bi girls were. I was having fun.

In 1992, I was laid-off from a good union job working for a parks and recreation department with a local municipality.

Around three months prior to my lay-off, I had filed a complaint against one of my managers for taking home city equipment for personal use. It was a really good job. I was 22 years-old and making the same kind of money that Dad was in his late forties working at a government civil service job painting speed bumps at Fort Lewis.

I always found it a bit hypocritical that we (along with most extreme right-wing Americans) hated the government, yet both Dad and I were working for the government. Robert Welch and the John Birch Society believed that government is always the enemy of the governed. I asked Dad if we were hypocrites. He said "no" and that city, county and state governments weren't the enemy. He said the real enemy was the enormous size of our federal government and many of the departments like the IRS, EPA, HUD and the Departments of Education, Energy and Commerce which should all be eliminated. I never bothered (because I didn't want to upset him) mentioning to him that he was in fact working for the federal government as a painter.

I was now living in downtown Tacoma after being laid-off. I was unemployed and quite active in the regional music scene playing in a band when I got involved with a small monthly music magazine in Tacoma. After volunteering with the magazine for about a month, some of the other staffers and I left and started our own alternative music magazine. I was the majority owner and publisher.

During this phase of my life, I was very much a part of the music and arts community in the Pacific Northwest. I had been a lead singer for an alternative rock band and had earrings, jet black hair and a very casual appearance. I certainly didn't dress or act like a young republican or anything remotely like that. Dad wasn't thrilled with my new lifestyle.

Every time there was a family gathering for a holiday or a birthday at my parent's house, he would always make wise cracks about my appearance. He'd call me Jesus for having long hair (longer than his bald head), even though my hair barely touched my shoulders. My hair wasn't too long. It just didn't meet his approval.

During one family gathering, he grabbed one of my earrings, pulled on it and said it was a handle. He told me that he was going to rip it out of my head. He never did, but his displeasure over my appearance kept him fired up and kept me annoyed. I tried staying away as much as I could. There wasn't much in my life at this time that made Dad proud of me, yet I was having a good time and enjoying modest success in the music and publishing industries. Life away from being his son was a lot of fun and very satisfying.

A few years after starting the music magazine, our company started an alternative weekly newspaper. The newspaper enjoyed great success. In 1999, our company was named the "Outstanding Business of the Year (company with 55 employees or less)" by the Tacoma-Pierce County Chamber of Commerce. We received a few national awards for our graphic design and content. The weekly paper had a heavy focus on culture, arts, music, community and politics.

Most alternative weekly newspapers in America are all quite liberal (i.e. *Village Voice*, etc.) and most, if not all of our writers had a heavy slant to the left. The writers were all college-educated (unlike me) and produced numerous articles on issues of homelessness, the environment and historic preservation.

Dad would sometimes call about things he had read or heard about in my newspaper. He was always negative and critical. I usually managed to change the subject to a different topic or make up a story on the spot about something we were going to publish that I knew would make him happy. We never did do any of those stories. I was blowing him off as there was no way I was going to allow his politics to interfere with my career and the success of my company.

Sometimes, however, during our editorial meetings (it was a very democratic process in choosing content), I'd suggest more conservative or libertarian-leaning story ideas and my suggestions, for the most part, didn't excite the group of journalists in the room.

I was critical of public tax dollars being used for downtown revitalization efforts and was adamant that private dollars were necessary for successful urban growth. I was very much leaning towards a conservative and pro-business point of view.

I was invited, along with a few other civic and government officials from Tacoma, to attend a Housing and Urban Development conference in Washington D.C. President Bill Clinton and Vice President Al Gore had established a new federal program called Empowerment Zones and Enterprise Communities which benefitted urban areas around the country. "These programs give some of the poorest Americans the opportunity to climb out of poverty under their own power, creating jobs that enable fathers and mothers to support their families and work their way up to the middle class," said Vice President Gore.

At the conference, I had my photo taken with Vice President Gore. I was proud of it. I showed the photo to my parents. They both laughed about the photo. It wasn't framed and hung on the wall. They weren't proud. Many years later, I heard that this photo made Dad angry and he felt betrayed. He's never said anything to me about it.

One day in 1998, after playing paintball and having a fantastic time out in the woods with a bunch of friends, I brought the idea of starting a paintball field to my parents. They had the land - forty rural acres now and they now lived alone on it as all four kids had moved out. Mom loved the prospect of having an endless supply of money to feed her unspoken gambling addiction and Dad was thrilled with the prospect of having dozens if not hundreds of people on his property shooting paintballs at each other playing war games. Plus, he had just retired early from his government job because of his bad back (which I'm sure had nothing to with the hundreds of cords of firewood that we sold in the eighties). Mom and Dad had the land, time, junk for making obstacles and I had the money, drive and know how to start and run the business.

That year, we opened the paintball field (which is still running to this day with different owners) and the business did what it needed to do. It gave Mom and Dad spending money and something to do, and it allowed me to be closer to my parents and fund my new hobby of playing paintball professionally. Eventually, the business became strong enough that it was paying my parents' mortgage and they both received cash under the table each week.

I was quite successful at the sport and business of paintball. I wrote for various paintball websites and magazines and owned a regional paintball tournament series for years. For two years, I was the captain of a semi-professional paintball team which won two world championships in Orlando, FL. Both of my parents were proud of me.

Early on, paintball was good for Mom, Dad and me as it brought us together on a weekly if not a daily basis, and for the most part we all got along. Going into business with my parents allowed them the opportunity to finally capitalize on their acreage without selling it off.

Because we were partners, there wasn't a lot of political talk or complaining about government or conspiracies. I was enjoying being around them and they were enjoying my presence as well. These were good times. Dad did complain a lot that Mom was skimming cash off the top for her daily visit to the local tribal casino. Mom would say she was going to Walmart, but everyone suspected that she was also swinging by a casino even if only for a few minutes.

During this period in the nineties, I was very busy running the newspaper, the paintball field and volunteering for a variety of nonprofit organizations.

I was also now married to a very liberal hippy chick (go figure). We got married in Las Vegas without any of my family members present. An Elvis impersonator gave her away. It was awesome. A year later we bought our first home in the suburbs and got a dog. Not long after that, we were getting ready to have a baby boy. Life was good.

There has only been one time I can recall Dad saying something genuine and honest to me. He had invited me to breakfast at a tiny restaurant a few months before my son was born. This was odd as the last time Dad invited me to meet him over a meal was in 1985 when he had me meet with a recruiter for the Washington Army National Guard. Needless to say, I was a bit skeptical and nervous.

He was already sitting in the booth when I walked into the restaurant. As I went to join him, I remember him looking very uncomfortable. I sat down and he was almost staring at me to make sure I fully understood the seriousness of what he was about to say. I couldn't stand the tension and actually thought about running out of the place.

After a little bit of small talk, he said, "You know the way I raised you isn't the way you'll want to raise your son." I remember looking at him thinking "well no shit." Instead I just said "Dad, you raised me just fine." We ordered breakfast and the conversation digressed. That was it. We never spoke of this again.

It wasn't okay how he raised me. There was no reason I could think of to challenge him at that moment over breakfast, and I certainly wasn't prepared to discuss my childhood with him.

I suspected his purpose in this meeting was supposed to be some sort of apology perhaps encouraged by his VA therapist to help deal with his guilt issues. A part of me was quite happy about this moment. I was feeling like this was a positive change for Dad and our relationship. Foolishly, I always think this way the few times he's done or said something halfway decent.

During this time, I received a personal invitation from a Tacoma city councilman to join an exclusive cigar and wine club in Tacoma. All the members unanimously voted me in. Members included many locally-elected officials, city department heads, some casino owners and other business leaders. The club met after hours every month at various establishments around Tacoma. One year we all went to the "Big Smoke" - a weekend in Las Vegas sampling cigars and partying sponsored by *Cigar Aficionado Magazine*.

The club didn't officially or legally exist. No minutes or records were maintained. Conversations mostly focused on the cigars we would smoke that evening or the liquor we drank. After a few drinks, however, the conversation always led to discussing other politicians that the group didn't like and what we could do to end their political careers or economic projects; things we felt would stifle economic growth in the Tacoma area and impact the bank accounts of various club members.

In my mind, I was a member of Tacoma's own Skull and Bones. I was an Insider. I never told Dad about the club.

Because of all of my activities and opinions about downtown Tacoma, a group of city councilmen and a few others began to groom me to run for a seat on the council. To appease and to impress them, I wrote a cover story on the then-current mayor titled, "Ten Things I Hate about the Mayor." They all loved it as none of them could stand the mayor. Dad loved it too because I had attacked a politician and a democrat. I wrote other articles as well supporting causes that club members were involved with or negative stories on topics that would win me more support. I was a good young pup kissing the right ass for my future political career.

My grooming to be a future Tacoma council member didn't last long however. One issue of our paper had a cover story focusing on the pollution taking place in Commencement Bay in the Puget Sound and how many of the larger businesses on the water were directly responsible for the pollution. One of my "friends" on the city council and in the club was upset that my newspaper ran the story. He was a developer and had plans to build on the waterway. He said the story made the waterway look like a cesspool and said that it could slow down development plans.

Truthfully, the waterway was a cesspool. The Thea Foss Waterway was one of America's worst polluted bodies of water and it needed to be cleaned up before new development should take place.

The day after the story was published, I received a phone call from another member of the club and I learned I was no longer having drinks with these councilmen and no longer in their club. I was out.

Even though these council members and business leaders weren't poor white trash like Dad, they were very much alike in the respect that you are either with them or against them.

By this time my appearance and lifestyle had changed. I was no longer active in the music scene. Sometimes I wore a suit to work and my hair was no longer jet black. I spent lunch meetings with executive directors of various non-profit organizations, elected officials and business people. I was a card-carrying member of the Rotary.

During all the years that I was publisher of the newspaper, I was quite active in many civic and community organizations including the Pierce County AIDS Foundation, the Chamber of Commerce, American Red Cross and many others. At one point, I was on the board of directors for Citizens for a Healthy Bay (a Puget Sound based environmental organization) and later become board president. I also served on the board of the Tacoma Actors Guild, which was one of the largest arts organizations in Tacoma. I became president of this organization as well.

Dad was aware of my activities and often tried to be critical. When he did, I would fight back and his lack of knowledge regarding the organizations forced him to remain silent. He always threw in the line, "it sure would be nice if you donated some of your free time and money to the John Birch Society." I never did of course.

My civic involvements weren't exactly the sort of mantras that the Birch Society and my father supported. In fact, most of the organizations that I was involved with were the complete opposite and I knew that I was going down a path of complete opposition to what my parents and my upbringing stood for. It felt good and it felt right. I knew that it angered Dad that I was president of the largest environmental organization in Tacoma and president of one of the largest arts organizations in Tacoma as well.

During this part of my life I learned many new lessons about politics beyond those taught during my upbringing. I had begun the difficult process of taking control of my choices and my life.

13 THE END

Immediately after the horror that happened during the morning of September 11th, 2001, I was I'm sure, like everyone. I was freaking out and scared to death about the future of America. I was worried that my family and I would no longer be free. I was worried that our lives would be in jeopardy. I was scared and miserable.

America didn't look the same after 9/11. This was real. It wasn't rhetoric or warnings coming from Dad or the John Birch Society. This was a serious attack on America and as far as I knew, it wasn't going to end until America was gone.

Further, what kind of person was I to have brought a new person into a world that was so messed up? Dad had spent his entire life warning me about this nightmare and now here I was with a little toddler and a wife in a world that was being destroyed in front of my own eyes. Dad had even warned me about having a child who might have to grow up living under a communist government.

It was a horrible feeling knowing I was responsible for this little kid's life and that the world wasn't looking so good. I felt hopeless. I asked myself why I had been so stupid. This wasn't fair to my son.

America was a different place in the days and weeks after 9/11. There were people from all over the world praying for America. It was surreal. There was constant despair. The television was repeatedly showing us video of the attacks and the aftermath. It was terrible. It was unbelievable. I began to think that Dad was right and this was the beginning of the end.

Later in the day on September 11th, after it appeared that the first wave of attacks were over, Dad said that "it" was happening and I knew what that meant. "This was just the beginning," he said. It didn't matter, according to Dad, who it was that perpetuated the attacks. What was important was that we knew these attacks happened because they were a part of the Conspiracy.

Foolishly, I believed this. I thought about how quickly I could drive my wife, son and I out to his property for safety and protection. I constantly wondered what the specific signs would be to indicate I should take such action to pack up and run. If I waited too long, we'd never make it. The drive was about forty-five minutes and if chaos was happening, we'd get stuck in traffic or there'd be government checkpoints set up and they'd stop us and we wouldn't make it. My mind was racing with thoughts of how to protect my family and myself.

A very compelling thing happened within days after 9/11. American flags were everywhere I went, and not just at car lots or in front of government buildings. There were American flags flying in front of businesses and homes - everywhere you looked, there was an American flag.

I would see a random guy on a street corner waving a huge flag and people honking at him and giving him a "thumbs up." If it had been September 10th, 2001, that same guy wouldn't have received the same "thumbs up" and friendly honking. People would have thought he was crazy or a homeless guy waiving an American flag on a street corner.

"It" never happened again or at least anything like what happened in America on September 11th, 2001.

Seeing the American flag everywhere brought feelings of calmness and happiness to me. It was as if America had awakened and was now unified and proud. I was incredibly proud to be my father's son in the immediate weeks following 9/11. He was by far the most patriotic person I ever knew and he had devoted his entire life to keeping America free. Now that we had this huge tragedy, more and more people seemed to be on the same page as Dad – at least with their public sense of patriotism.

The events of 9/11 had a profound effect on my intellectual reasoning. I kept regressing and found comfort in the things he taught me when I was younger, despite knowing he was nuts. Part of me agreed with him. It was a constant tugging between reality and the paranoia that Dad had seeded inside my brain. It was exhausting to struggle with trying to decide what was or wasn't real.

I knew what was going on in America. Dad was right, I thought.

"It" was happening and Dad was ready. I believed I was lucky that he was.

Dad and I had another conversation a few days later about how the American flag was now cool. Before, it wasn't exactly a cool thing for people to walk around waving an American flag. In fact, patriotism barely existed in America in the seventies, eighties or nineties except during the Olympic Games. Typically, the only people who would proudly display their flag were old vets who would fly it in the front of their homes and occasionally businesses once a year on Flag Day.

Dad said that in time people will go back to being "blind to what's really going on." I knew what he meant, but I wasn't sure what he implied by alleging that flying an American flag indicated that the eyes of my fellow citizens were no longer blind to the Communist Conspiracy. It appeared to me that they were just trying to rebuild a sense of freedom and patriotism in this country by rallying around the flag.

Even though I was getting very close with Dad again, I'd still get irritated by some of the ridiculous, mean and useless things he'd say. Being critical of other people had always been something that Dad excelled in, but it seemed overly mean to be critical of other well-meaning Americans at that time.

The reason I called Dad, the exact reason I had called a hundred times before and after, was to let him know that things were getting better in America. All of his hard work and dedication was worth it and finally paying off. I wanted him to be proud of himself. I wanted him to know that I was proud of him and proud that he was my father. I wanted to give him kudos and hopefully a sense of real peace so he could actually live freely and enjoy his life. I also wanted him to know that he was a major part of the reason America was getting better.

Every time I did this and every time I've done this throughout my entire life, the results were always consistent - he was negative, contemptuous and suspicious about things getting better. He'd say for every good thing that happened in America today, four bad things happened that they wouldn't tell us about or that we didn't know about. He said it was part of the Conspiracy's plan to make us relax when a good thing happened and not know what was really going on. He said not to be fooled by people standing around waving flags and that their behavior was exactly what the Conspiracy wanted so they could make advancements in their destruction of America while we weren't paying attention.

Dad, along with thousands and thousands of other paranoid Americans believe that 9/11 was an inside job ultimately perpetuated by the grand Communist Conspiracy. Still, he hates Muslims for their role in carrying out the attacks. "The terrorists are working for the communists," Dad said. I'd just nod my head in partial agreement. Dad never could explain or defend his theories, but he would push them on anyone who would listen. If challenged, he would attack with name calling. This was a common response to questions directed at him. He would warn of a cover up of the truth, but without any supporting evidence of his claims. "You can't believe anything that you see on the news or read in the paper from the mainstream media," he'd always say.

Dad never created any conspiracy theories on his own other than local obsessions with neighbors stealing firewood, tools or other things.

He never had any proof or facts, just a hunch that someone was always out to get him.

14 YOU CAN'T ALWAYS GET WHAT YOU WANT

For a variety of reasons including wanting to get some distance from my parents, in 2004, I moved my family about one hundred twenty miles farther away to the Washington coast. This move was enough to reduce the chance of frequent interactions with them.

A few years later after working through my own therapy and reading numerous self-help books, my therapist suggested my struggles in life existed because I hadn't forgiven Dad for my childhood experiences with him. I had spent most of my life hating him and I needed to move on. I carried a lot of anger around and it was preventing me from being a good person. My therapist encouraged me to forgive him and get on with my life. He said I needed to do this to be free of my childhood anger, and that I should talk to my parents.

After that session, I called my parents and asked if I could come over and talk to them. Mom asked, "Talk about what?"

I said I needed to talk about some things and would be there in a couple of hours.

When I arrived, they were sitting in their living room and I joined them. There was no small talk. I told them about my behavior, my anger and my honest feelings about my childhood and the impact it's had on my life. I told them I forgave them for their roles in my childhood and I loved them both.

They downplayed my issues and concerns and said I should quit therapy. They said the reason I was so successful with many of my endeavors was because of how they raised me. They took credit for my achievements and said I shouldn't dwell on the negative stuff and that I actually had a great childhood. More than anything, they were concerned about the fact that I was in therapy. They couldn't understand why I needed it. They thought it was silly and ridiculous.

I slept on their couch that night and left in the morning.

Even though the visit was a complete failure, I was in a good mood and proud of myself for having this talk with my parents. I was in denial over what had happened during our meeting. I was feeling as if I had finally stood up to them and had an honest conversation. I told my wife and my therapist about the night, how uncomfortable it was, and how liberating it felt.

Not too many years later, Mom divorced Dad and eventually married one of his friends who had more money than him and turned a blind eye to her gambling addiction. Not long after that the paintball business was sold and the three of us were no longer business partners.

Mom called the day she left Dad to tell me she was divorcing him. I told her I was proud of her and that if I could divorce him, I would too. She said, "I know honey. He's a horrible person, but he has a disease."

She shared a lot about their marital issues and how Dad had cheated on her for decades including a time not long after I was born.

Mom was scared for her life when she left Dad. She went on a month-long trip south to California to visit relatives and never even talked to him. She left him a note saying she was divorcing him and that she was going on a trip and he wouldn't be able to find or talk to her. She was afraid of what he might do to her and her new boyfriend. I knew she went to California (because she told me) to visit with her mother and her siblings, but I didn't know exactly where she would be.

Dad never bothered trying to find her, but he did ask me a few times if I had talked to her recently or if I knew where she was or who she was with. I told him I didn't know.

Dad was devastated when he found out she was divorcing him even though he had spent his entire marriage complaining to everyone about her. Dad certainly wouldn't have left Mom, but he easily would have spent the rest of his life complaining about how miserable she made him.

Dad didn't handle the divorce very well. I talked with him on the phone a few times after Mom left trying to provide him with some comfort. He wouldn't share or discuss much about what he was doing or how he was feeling. Mom had exposed Dad as a loser and he was humiliated by this. I asked him about all of the cheating on Mom one time. All he said was, "is that what she's telling you?" I told him I heard something about it and was just wondering. He accused me of taking sides in their divorce. When I asked him what made him think that, he said "I know you are." I didn't argue with him.

To this day Dad won't fess up about his role in the collapse of their marriage. He blames everything on Mom. He's still in denial. Two years after the divorce he was still angry and felt betrayed.

Like Mom, Dad embraced the role of the traditional American family and when Mom left, that was over. His happy American family was no more. He couldn't stand it.

Dad was so irate about his divorce that one day while I was talking with him on the phone trying to comfort him he said, "I hope your wife and son both leave you so you'll know how this feels!" I hung up on him. He never called back and never apologized for saying what he did.

A few years after they were divorced, Mom and I were having a conversation on the phone when the subject of my frustrations with Dad came up again. Out of the blue, Mom says, "your father loves you, but just doesn't know how to show it honey."

She's been saying this my entire life.

I said, "really Mom? Why do you keep saying that? Is it because you think he actually loved you for all those years and didn't know how to show that either?"

She hung up and we've hardly talked since.

I think she only says this because deep inside she knows he's never loved anyone including her, except maybe his mother and Claymore, his dead Rottweiler. Mom is still in complete denial that she wasted over forty years with a man who never loved her. By claiming "he just doesn't know how to show it" - even two years after divorcing him - she is still lying for him, to herself and to me.

That day and that conversation was the last time she lied to me. From that day forward, I was done having conversations with her. I had finally found a sense of peace and acceptance in knowing that Dad actually doesn't love me and that's okay. Trying to make someone love you when they just don't is an unbearable situation, especially if it's one or even both of your parents. Mom's insistence that he does love me showed me that she is also incapable of love and honesty with me. She was lying. This was the day I gave up on my mother.

Sometimes, however, I still long for a real relationship with them. In the fall of 2012, my wife, son and I were near Dad's house and we swung by for an unannounced visit. Dad wasn't home, but in front of his unpermitted shop sat a huge pile of political signs from two different democrat candidates for local state offices.

I saw the political signs piled up on the ground and knew why they were there and who put them there. I immediately felt sick to my stomach. "What a piece of crap," I said to myself. I was disgusted to think my sixty-something year-old father is the kind of person who drives around taking down political signs. My wife and son saw the signs too and knew why they were sitting there.

I took a couple of photos of the signs with my iPhone and we left. A few days later, I decided to call the campaign headquarters of the politicians on the signs to tell them that their signs were piled up at a house that is owned by a registered member of the Republican Party and a chapter leader of the John Birch Society. When I called the first

117

headquarters, a lady answered and when she said hello I hung up. I never did speak to Dad about the signs or our visit. I haven't been to Dad's property since.

When I called to tell Dad that Republican President Candidate Ron Paul was going to be on the *Tonight Show* during the 2012 Presidential Election, he said it didn't matter because Ron Paul couldn't get elected. I said "that might be true. But his message will get out to more people and that would be a good thing for America."

Dad reiterated that it didn't matter anymore and a vote for Ron Paul would be a waste because there's no way he'd win. In his mind, it would be a win for the Conspiracy because it would help Obama get reelected.

"Vote for Mitt Romney," he said. "He's our only hope to get that nigger commie out of there."

Dad was serious - scary serious. His tone was vicious. I was just trying to be supportive of him and once again hoping we might have a decent conversation.

President Obama has upset a lot of people in America. To people like my father it's not because of what he has or hasn't done as president, but mainly, of course, because he's black.

Dad didn't hold back when talking about Obama. We didn't discuss who I had voted for in 2008 and 2012 and I can only assume that he thought I voted for Ron Paul. Of course, that's who I told him I voted for.

There was no reason to discuss this with him honestly. I told him what he wanted to hear. Most of the time I just said "wow" or "that's crazy" to him or I would casually try to change the subject. Challenging Dad's statements was a pointless pursuit.

The advent of social media has created an entirely new level of frustration and embarrassment about being my parents' son. When your parents are actively spreading their hate on Facebook, it doesn't matter how far away you live from them. Their level of enthusiasm for sharing hate-filled messages behind their computers is even higher than it ever was in person. Mom rarely said anything hateful or racist in person. Now that she's on Facebook, she has no problem sharing a meme displaying her support of the confederate flag and "if it offends you, well then too bad."

Their hate, racism and ignorance are now on my laptop and smart phone. When Mom and Dad share their hate on Facebook, it's actually worse than hearing it firsthand because others see it as well. Facebook in particular, has enabled a lot of people to share things on their computer they might never do in person out of fear of being labeled a racist, an idiot or a jerk. Many of my high school classmates are "friends" of my Mom and Dad and get to see just how ignorant, racist and pathetic my parents are.

In July, 2013, I received an invitation from Dad to be his friend on Facebook. Before I clicked on "accept," I looked at his activity.

What I found was shocking and ridiculous. Dad "liked" a photo of some twenty something year-old who dressed very much like a stripper. I clicked on her photo and sure enough, she was a stripper and also a topless barista. Not only that, but she was "friends" with my father!

I immediately called Dad. "Why are you friends with a stripper on Facebook?"

He said he wasn't friends with a stripper.

I told him about the girl on his Facebook wall and how her profile showed that she worked as a topless barista and a dancer at a strip club.

Dad said he didn't know how Facebook worked and didn't know what she was doing on there. He also said he had no idea who the girl was and they weren't "friends." He said he'd figure it out.

I said to him, "Dad, you either friended her or she friended you and either way, you are her 'friend' on Facebook."

He said "this is bullshit."

I explained to him that all of his grandchildren, his children and all of his friends and probably the entire world can see that he's friends with a stripper and this isn't a great thing for his grandchildren to see and certainly doesn't look good for a member of the John Birch Society. "What are you doing?" I asked.

The conversation got really heated at this point and Dad finally yelled, "Well, at least I don't have any democrat friends on Facebook!" He then hung up. Within a few minutes, Dad and the stripper were no longer friends - at least on Facebook.

Needless to say, I declined Dad's invite to be "friends."

This appeared on Dad's Facebook a month later: "If YOU so called Patriots would do YOUR civic duties, such as regularly communicating with your Congressman and your 2 U.S. Senators, we would most likely not be on the brink of living under a Communist Dictatorship. It's still not too late, no matter what the weak-kneed, spineless naysayers say, including 'Pay your taxes, don't complain or protest. You'll get your name on a list. Turn in your guns. Who needs them? You don't hunt anymore.' Digest this quote from Samuel Adams. 'If ye love wealth better than liberty, the tranquility of servitude better than the animating contest of freedom, go home from us in peace. We ask not your counsels or arms. Crouch down and lick the hands which feed you. May your chains set lightly upon you, and may posterity forget that ye were our countrymen.'"

No one "liked" Dad's post and within a few days he deleted it.

It's almost as if he has these bi-polar rages and shares them on Facebook. Then days later he logs back in and sees his nonsense and deletes it all.

Knowing how Dad's brain works, I figured he deleted his post over fear that "they" were watching.

When I first read his post, I thought he was directing the post at me. I never did ask.

Dad posted this on his personal Facebook wall in January, 2014 – the day after Pete Seeger died: "Pete Seeger died? Let the moaning and wailing begin! This old Communist Party revolutionary was cut from the same cloth as 'kindly' old Nelson Mandela. Both Communist Party activists, and both revered by our media and government. Good riddance.

Don't believe me? Google "Pete Seeger communist."

His post was public so anyone on Facebook could see it. At the time, Dad had 126 Facebook friends and fifteen of those were mutual friends including some of his grandchildren. I monitored his wall every day just waiting to see if anyone had liked it. Four days later, no one had "liked" it and Dad finally deleted his post.

I fully realize that Dad's hateful post regarding Seeger's death likely didn't have an effect on anyone other than me. This post, his message to the world, shows that Dad is still as hateful as ever.

When I first saw his post, it filled me with rage, anger and complete embarrassment that he's my father. All his Facebook friends who know I'm his son know that he raised me to be just like him. The thought of anyone thinking that I'm anything like him horrifies and embarrasses me.

I didn't know much about Pete Seeger other than when I was younger I knew he was a commie and the guy that wrote the song "This Land is Your Land," which according to Dad was a song that promoted communism in America.

After I read Dad's post, I was angry and realized that I actually knew nothing about Pete Seeger and decided to do some research. Pete Seeger was an American and a Christian who regularly attended church with his wife until he died. He served in the US Army from 1942 to 1945. He was a folk singer and an activist who sought positive change in America. Seeger was a patriot who loved America and the freedom it stands for more than my father who spits on his grave out of hate and ignorance. Pete Seeger tried to make America a better place for everyone. If it meant joining the Communist Party and then later quitting (after learning of Stalin's atrocities in the '50s), Seeger wasn't afraid to admit he was wrong and he did. He did no harm to America. He loved this country and simply wanted it to be better place for everyone.

Of course it may not be a big deal to any of my relatives or peers from high school what my parents do on social media, but to me it's shameful, embarrassing, pathetic and horrific. I have since unfriended Mother and have blocked both of them on Facebook. At least this way I don't have to see what they're doing.

In 2014, I guess Dad was doing some house cleaning and found a copy of the newspaper that published my letter about our republic when I was in high school. Dad sent it to me with a sticky note attached that said "so proud of you."

In doing so, Dad probably thought he was doing a nice thing or at least he thought he could make it look like he was doing a nice thing. In reality, Dad was taking a shot at me. He was reminding me of how good of a son I used to be. He doesn't approve of me not being a right-wing extremist in the war against the Conspiracy and Obama. He thinks of me as a failure, and sending that letter to me was his way of reminding me of that. I threw the newspaper clipping and his note in the trash.

15 FORTUNATE SON 2.0

In June 2015, still trying to make sense of things, I sent Dad a few texts asking him exactly what day his dad died and exactly what day he came home from the war in Vietnam.

A few nights before, my wife and I watched *Coming Home*, the 1978 Vietnam-era, anti-war and award-winning movie starring Jane Fonda and John Voight.

I had never seen this movie before and had avoided watching movies like this because Dad said such films were anti-war and un-American (and of course because it was a Jane Fonda movie).

In the movie, while Fonda's husband is in Vietnam, she falls in love with the paralyzed soldier at home played by John Voight. Eventually Fonda cheats on her husband with Voight.

At this moment in time, I had an invigorating thought, stopped the movie and said to my wife, "Mom had an affair when Dad was in Vietnam and he's not really my dad!"

We discussed this for a few minutes and I had this beautiful hope that I wasn't my father's biological son. This made so much sense to me. I was excited, curious and relieved.

I don't look anything like my Dad. He's short, fat and bald. I'm tall with a full head of hair and not fat. We have nothing in common. We don't like each other. I've spent my entire life trying to get this guy to love me and he won't. He doesn't, I'm thinking, because I'm not really his son. Mom must have had an affair when Dad was in Vietnam.

Everything about my relationship with Dad made so much sense to me now, for the first time.

I did my best to pay attention to the rest of the movie, but my mind was focused on this potential revelation. I started thinking that maybe Dad wasn't even stateside nine months before I was born. I wondered if Dad knew about this. I figured he probably did. Maybe this is why he had always been so mean - particularly to Mom and me?

He must have known that I wasn't his biological son and knew that Mom had an affair and a baby while he was gone at war. I was his bastard child and he only stayed with Mom and agreed to raise me because he desperately tried to have, in his mind, the perfect American family.

Maybe this was why Dad had cheated on Mom - to get even and pay her back? Maybe this was why he raised me so differently from my siblings.

I wondered what my real father looked like and what he did for a living. Did he have other children? Was he tall and not fat like me? I had all these questions running around inside my head. Did Dad know who my biological father was?

I was weaving my new reality.

All I needed was proof and I didn't have the nerve to ask Dad and didn't really want to talk to Mom about this. I thought about hiring a private investigator to get Dad's DNA to see if we were a match. I looked up some ancestry websites, but they didn't help. It became an obsessive pursuit.

I didn't know exactly when my Dad's dad died, so I needed this information first.

I sent Dad a text message: "Hey, what month and year did your dad die? I was just wondering."

My phone rang within seconds of sending the text. It was Dad. I didn't take his call. He didn't leave a message and I didn't call back. I was intrigued.

He responded to my text two hours later, "Dad died 10/12/67 when I was in 'Nam. Why?"

I texted back a few hours later, "Just thinking about it. I thought you were back when he died."

He didn't respond. Two days later and without a response, I re-sent the same text and he still didn't respond.

I called him a few hours later. He answered and said he wanted to know why I was asking questions like these.

I said, "I was just thinking about how I don't really know anything about your dad (my grandfather) and was curious."

Dad said he came back home from Vietnam a day after his dad died in the hospital and remained stateside permanently (almost one full year before I was born). He didn't mention anything about his entire platoon being killed and I didn't ask.

So, this wasn't good news for my theory, assuming Dad was telling me the truth. I wondered if he was going to tell Mom that I was on to their secret in the event he was lying.

I was completely frustrated. I thought for sure now that I wasn't his biological son and the thought of that filled me with joy and happiness. All the embarrassment, hostility and ridicule that I had lived with were all slipping away during the few weeks that I thought he wasn't my real dad.

On the way to a therapy session, I called my favorite uncle in California and shared with him what was going on. We discussed the matter extensively and he said he knew nothing about Mom having an affair before I was born and that he didn't believe that she did.

After my session discussing this matter with my therapist, I called Mom for the first time in over a year on my way home.

"Hi," I said.

"Hi," she said.

"Did you cheat on Dad or were you having an affair in January or February 1968?"

She said, "What?"

"There's no way that I could actually be Dad's biological son," I said.

She laughed and said, "Sorry. But your dad is your dad."

I knew she was telling the truth. I was devastated and speechless. I could sense the rare honesty in her tone.

She asked me how my book was coming along. She's known for years I was writing this book and told me it was stupid to do so. I told her I hoped to have it done soon and she should watch for it on the *New York Times Best Sellers* list.

After our very brief conversation, I stared at myself in the rear view mirror of my truck for what seemed like ten minutes. I was staring into my eyes to see if I could see a resemblance. I could see him in my eyes after a while. I looked down at my short stalky fingers and they looked like his short fat fingers. I was defeated. I was his son. We share the same blood.

Two very good friends of mine lost their fathers in the summer of 2015. They took it very hard. They were very close to their fathers who had loved them without shame. Each of their fathers was adored by all of their children, family and friends. They had made significant positive impacts in the lives of those around them and the two men had lived full lives. Both of their fathers are sorely missed.

I couldn't relate to either one of them. I could only imagine what it might feel like to have such a father, or such parents for that matter. It was yet another sad revelation for me. I couldn't empathize. I could only sympathize and I admired their feelings of loss and sadness.

The last time I saw Dad was at Good Samaritan Hospital in Puyallup, Washington late in the summer of 2015. We were notified by my youngest sister that my other sister (who's a few years younger than I am, but in her forties and has a long history of crack addiction) was pregnant. She didn't know she was pregnant, but was now in the ICU and might not survive.

When we arrived a few hours later, Dad was in her room along with my sister-in-law and my pregnant sister's two teenagers. The doctors said she had a staph infection and the baby had to be removed or they both could die. They later transferred them to Tacoma General Hospital where my newest niece was born weighing just over a pound. This baby would have to spend the next three to four months in the hospital before she would be released. We found out later that night that my sister had MRSA and we were all exposed to it. No one contracted the disease from her after the visit, but the risk was there.

The next day, I heard from my sister-in-law after she spent some one-on-one time driving my Dad around (apparently he doesn't drive much anymore). She had listened to him cry and complain that neither one of his boys love him. She didn't know what to say to him, but encouraged him to call his sons and tell them how he felt. He never did.

I called Dad later that day in the evening and asked how he felt about being a grandpa again. His response was "Oh yeah."

I asked him if he knew who the father of his new granddaughter was. He said some guy named Scott.

"Does Scott have a job with insurance?" I asked.

"No," he said.

"So how are they going to pay for all of the hospital bills or is our socialistic health care system going to take care of it?" I asked.

He said "Right. You know who's paying for this" and I snapped back at him, "So much for individual responsibility and all that other stuff," referencing a portion of the Birch Society's motto. He said nothing.

"So where does this Scott live?" I asked him.

"In his camper in my driveway with your sister," he said sounding frustrated.

I laughed out loud and said, "Well at least she's not on Section 8 housing anymore.

He said nothing.

Dad said he had to go. A friend of his was at the front door with a bucket of chicken from KFC and he said he had to eat it before it got cold. I asked, "Where's the nearest KFC to your house?" "Around twenty minutes away," he replied. "Well it's probably already cold," I said. He replied "I don't think so. Catch you later," and hung up. It wouldn't surprise me if we never talk again.

I sent both of my parents a text greeting just before Christmas in 2015 that said "Happy Holidays" with a cute photo on it. Neither responded and neither one of them wished me or my family, which includes their grandson, a "Merry Christmas" or a "Happy New Year." Oh well.

16 OLD MAN

Congratulations Dad! The war against the International Communist Conspiracy is over and you've won! America is a safer place because of your determination and ruthless efforts to destroy the evil satanic forces out to take away our freedoms. Your children and grandchildren will all live in the home of the brave without having to be slaves in communist prison camps. You've spent half a century fighting this war and at what cost, Dad? That's for you decide.

Maybe when you're dead, just maybe you'll be able to look back and see you wasted your life, lost time with your family and your relationships fighting an imaginary enemy and war. The Communist Conspiracy was as real as the boogie man. Matter of fact old man, you propagated a real conspiracy - which was that there was a Communist Conspiracy when, in fact, no conspiracy ever existed.

The rich scumbags who created the Communist Conspiracy are much like the guy on the bus who yells "who farted!?!" Reasonable people know that he's the one who farted, except for you and all the other panicked "patriots" who are out to save America. You believed that the kid asking really wasn't the one who committed the act. Everyone but you and your extremist friends knows that if you fart in a public place, you never ask who did it.

The Communist Conspiracy was a lie - a vicious lie created by those Americans you admired who are greedy, shallow and full of contempt, fear and hate. These bastards were only afraid to lose their money, power and the world they created for themselves with their wealth and influence. Your heroes - The Koch's, Robert Welch, Joseph McCarthy, Ted Cruz and David Duke - have all been incredibly successful in corrupting your mind and soul. You were a pawn in the Vietnam War and you've been a pawn in the war against the Conspiracy here at home. You're a grunt who doesn't question orders and does what you're told. "Good Christians, like slaves and soldiers, ask no questions," Jerry Falwell said.[1]

You're such a good low-level grunt, Dad. You're just as dumb, white, poor and angry today as you were in the sixties. You couldn't just one time question the idiotic reasoning behind most of what the extreme right-wing said was true. You were a perfect soldier in the anti-intellectual fight against humanity, reason and freedom.

Any crackpot conspiracy theory that comes across to the average person as a crackpot conspiracy theory will come across as the truth to Dad. It's because he's intellectually lazy and any conspiracy theory that has an easy explanation makes sense to him.

He'll buy it, sell it, share it and put the bumper sticker on the back of his truck. If it comes from the NRA, the John Birch Society or the plethora of Tea Party organizations and offshoots these days, Dad will believe it as the truth every time. And, if there's someone to blame (Clintons, Obama, Gore, the Illuminati, Pelosi, the White House, the rich, etc.), and there always is, he'll attack.

Organizations such as the Council of Foreign Relations, the Trilateral Commission, the United Nations, the International Monetary Fund, NATO, NAFTA, UNICEF and the World Bank are held in contempt. The Birchers label these organizations as part of the Conspiracy. They attack most branches of the US government as integral parts as well. According to them, the IRS, EPA, FEMA, ATF, CIA, FBI, TSA, Homeland Security, the Departments of HUD, Education, Commerce, Treasury, Transportation and others exist solely to assist the Conspiracy and destroy America. Public schools, arts organizations, sports teams and leagues, contemporary music, film and television exist only to distract us from acknowledging that the Conspiracy even exists at all.

Throughout the years they have "attacked and criminalized organizations such as the ACLU even though the ACLU has actually defended the John Birch Society."[2] They rejected Planned Parenthood, the United Way, Red Cross, the Humane Society and others, not because they disagreed with their mission or opposed it, but only because these organizations weren't fighting the Communist Conspiracy and took money that could have gone to the John Birch Society.

Dad was adamantly opposed to the existence of the federal government (not the military though) because of, (in his mind) their intrusions and confiscations of our basic rights and freedoms guaranteed by the Constitution. He saw the feds as a pawn to the global elite. His hatred level wasn't just based on their willingness to hand over our sovereignty. It was also based on the premise that the federal government protected feminist women, blacks along with other minorities, gay people, the environmentalists and others he believed were out to get him.

This, he believed, was that they were destroying his status as the almighty entitled white male (like each and every one of our founding fathers....). The federal government, he believed, was doing everything it could to ruin his life as a white American man.

Dad is an apologetic; always on the defense of anyone or anything that opposes him. He's a one-way conversation that never turns into a discussion or argument. He speaks, in his mind, the absolute truth with no possibility of being wrong. Dad's interest is only in getting you to believe his ideology and then for you to follow suit. The reason Dad won't sit down and have a rational mature discussion with anyone who isn't like him is because he can't. He knows exactly what he's saying and what it means, but when presented with other useful and factual information, he'll pass it off as lies or excuses created simply for the sole purpose of countering his information. If you don't believe his story or theory, it's because you're brainwashed or just stupid.

He's like a pastor of sorts. He'll threaten you that your freedoms and liberties will be gone real soon if you don't do something to stop the evil. This tactic has been used on me by Dad my entire life and was also employed on me a long time ago by a Baptist pastor who told me that I was going to go to hell unless I went to Church every Sunday. I never saw that pastor again.

I think the reason Dad believed everything he read or was told by the extreme right-wing media was because he wanted to feel intelligent without having to study or put in the work. Believing in conspiracy theories is a form of therapy for him - it justifies his existence on the losing side of society and it helps his ego. He also wants to be "right."

The ability for Dad to believe that what he's being told is the absolute truth without evidence, facts or reasoning is easy for him. Because he completely trusts his source, (the John Birch Society), he doesn't have to consider whether anything he is being fed has validity. "Obama is a Satanic Muslim who serves the devil and ISIS. He only goes to a Christian church to make us think that he doesn't love Satan or ISIS when in fact, he really does." This false quote makes perfect sense to my Dad and he's now comforted with what he knows to be true (even though it's not).

If a different media source conflicts with Dad's beliefs, he'll dismiss it without examination or consideration. "CNN is owned by commies!" The best way for him and other Birchers to be good pawns in the extreme right-wing is to just believe everything the extreme right-wing tells them. This way they're always right. And, when the conspiracy theory is proven totally false, they have no obligation whatsoever to believe any new evidence. The extreme right-wing and Dad believe what they are going to believe regardless of any accurate factual, reality-based information. Their simple, silly, yet evil suspicions and mean-spirited accusations are their truth. They'll blame it on the source that discredits their theory. "CNN is owned by commies!"

Dad's bizarre conspiracies and the other conspiracies being fed to him are the glue that holds together his beliefs. It is also what holds together the entire extreme right-wing conservative movement. The fear, denial and rage that exist within the movement keep them together. Whether it's the John Birchers, the KKK, the Tea Partiers, the Nazi's, the fundamental Christians, the militia groups, or the open carry nut jobs - they are all fearful, inaccurate and united.

There is no known cure for stupidity or paranoia. When grownups are afraid of boogiemen, they'll never be able to use reason or logic. We'll never be able to convince them of the self-evident truths placed in front of them. They'll see it, but they'll interpret it as something they are being tricked into seeing. Facts will be rejected.

"Fear is the path to the dark-side. Fear leads to anger. Anger leads to hate. Hate leads to suffering."[3] Perhaps Master Yoda was referring to our Communist Conspiracy when he said this to Anakin in *Star Wars*. Every paranoid right-wing nut job has become the way they are because of fear. They tune in to their extreme right-wing news sources for affirmations, pop two Percocet pills, have a few shots of Canadian whiskey and get mad as hell - like my Dad.

They believe the Communist Conspiracy in America exists because collectivism and spreading the wealth doesn't benefit them. They distrust other individuals who are compassionate, kind and giving. They call them liberals, socialists, humanists, pussies and other names, because those "liberals" want to make the entire world a better place – not just America.

Dad, has it occurred to you that the spreading of the wealth you object to ensures that our government sends you your checks every month? Do you realize it also ensures that your drug-addicted daughter has a drug treatment facility to attend? Spreading the wealth ensures that you can continue to receive medical treatment and drugs for your bad back.

Spreading the wealth means your new welfare-dependent grandchild has a chance at survival. Spreading the wealth doesn't mean handing over what minimal taxes you've ever paid to minority drug users who refuse to get a job Dad. If it wasn't for those "spreading the wealth," you would likely be homeless or already dead.

Entitlement is the reason a Communist Conspiracy in America exists. Be it the excessively wealthy or the dirt poor of the extreme right - both share in heinous entitlement issues. The Birchers believe America exists only for them and other people like them. They believe they are being cheated, robbed and offended every time this country does something beneficial for anyone who is not like them.

"For our enemy is the Communists, and we do not intend to lose sight of that fact for a minute. We are fighting the Communists - nobody else. Being fully aware of the imminence and horror of the danger we face from that source, we have no intention of being distracted by the carping of our friends, or of those who should be our friends and we hope will be our friends in time. For if we do there is entirely too much likelihood – as we have already said elsewhere and many times - that in a few short years we shall all be hanging from the same lamp posts, while Communist terror reigns around us," said Robert Welch in early 1958 in his *Blue Book.*

He never did define a "few short years," but he wrote this well over a half century ago.

Dad is convinced that the reason I'm not hanging from a lamp post surrounded by communist terror is because of all of the efforts of the many great patriotic Americans in the John Birch Society. The last thing he'd tell you is that you should join the John Birch Society – unless you hate freedom of course.

Dad, you've spent your entire life identifying and aligning yourself as a patriotic American. You've stood firm with your values and never backed down from the ideals you perpetuate. You always won political debates (to your own satisfaction anyhow) and admired yourself for your achievements. You never compromised. You'd fight to the death over your issues. You were firm, even when it wasn't politically-correct (which was always.) You thought your narrowmindedness was a sign of integrity. You slept well at night and paid no attention to the consequences of your extremism. You're an American, Dad - a proud, stupid American fighting a non-existent enemy in a war that isn't real. I'm sure grandma is rolling in her grave.

Martin Luther King and John F Kennedy weren't communists or traitors Dad. Neither was Eisenhower, Clinton or Obama. Russia and the United Nations were never out to get us and take our land. Pete Seeger wanted the best for you, Dad. Jane Fonda wasn't out to betray you. She went to Vietnam to encourage an end to that stupid war that killed all your buddies and ruined your life.

History is littered with repeating stories of people who lost their mind, their decency, and basic humanity when they felt that their existence or place in society was threatened. Since the election of Barrack Obama, the ugly in America has come out into the forefront. It's loud, ugly, makes no apologies and has no shame for its ignorance and contempt. It's an ugly that doesn't care if Obama has done a good job or not. It doesn't matter.

Before Obama was elected in 2008, my dad was still a kook in the closet that no one took seriously. He was a joke. He was an idiot. He was your crazy uncle type who believed in all kinds of things that couldn't be proven.

Hatred, fear, and paranoia are gaining traction in America. Dad is no longer just a closet kook and crazy old man. He's among millions of Americans these days who have forgotten what it means to be free, to be decent, and to let other Americans who aren't like them enjoy the same freedoms they relish. Dad is no longer a crazy, harmless wacko nut job. He's firmly aligned with the likes of Ted Cruz, Donald Trump, Ben Carson, Glen Beck, Alex Jones and Ammon Bundy (the Oregon militia leader).

These people and the organizations to which you dedicated yourself, took advantage of your anger, Dad. You couldn't stand the concept of another person, not like you, sharing the freedoms to which every American is entitled. Your hatred for gays, immigrants, minorities, foreigners, environmentalists, hippies and liberals has fed the cause of the extreme right and done nothing for you except make you poorer and even more pathetic.

You believed in "the Conspiracy" so much that you offered up your first-born child to fight in your war. You brainwashed and withheld love and affection because your warrior child needed to be tough and headstrong to achieve your victory. I was your offering in this radical, ridiculous fight. You threw me away and then, when I struggled with trying to obey your nightmare, you rejected me. When I eventually challenged you on your hypocrisy, you cut me off.

Barely anything that you have ever done has benefited you or your family. You're a waste, a pathetic waste of life, Dad. You've enjoyed nothing except your pills, your booze, your conspiracies and the sound of your own voice.

I have despised you. I have hated myself for loving you. I have hated that you're my father. I've been embarrassed that you're my father. I have hated myself for loving you and for living much of my life trying to get you to love me. The connection we have is tiny - it's of blood and the thought that I can't do anything about that has at times made me sick, but I know it is time to put this all away because I don't want to spend any more of my life hating like you. I don't want to hate even if I am hated.

17 WHERE IT'S AT

I shudder to think what sort of person I would be today had I not escaped the influence of my upbringing. I've always known that there was something wrong with my parents. Had I not come to understand this, I'd likely be dead, in prison or a right-wing extremist politician.

Dad always warned me about the future of America and said that action was likely going to be necessary to keep our country free. If I had continued living under his roof, I might have blown up buildings, killed certain people or sought political office to make him proud and to save our Republic.

Only in the past few years have I been able to look back over the life I've lived so far and seriously examine my childhood. I have had to come to terms with the thoughts, decisions and actions that were a direct reflection of what my parents taught me as a young boy. This examination has been stressful, unsettling and has brought to the surface a lot of deep-seated anger which I've carried most of my life. I never understood it at all until recently.

I first began writing my thoughts down in 2011 after getting extremely frustrated with both of my parents when visiting them. It came from witnessing Dad's ridiculous behavior. It would also happen during conversations on the phone with either of them. Mom would often defend him (even after they were divorced) or would tell me to just ignore him and put my frustrations aside. Often she wouldn't listen to me and would simply tell me to "knock it off."

This journal I began writing was therapeutic as it allowed me to vent about the nonsense that came out of Dad's mouth.

Sometimes, I'd just sit at my computer and type my memories from when I was younger. One story or memory would remind me of another and I'd continue to write when it felt necessary. After I'd read what I had written, I'd often get angry and shocked and then I'd share my stories with my wife and others. Most were appalled by what I told them of my childhood experiences and what continued throughout my life as a result of being my father's son.

During the course of writing this book, I made my mother aware of it and she said it was stupid, a waste of time and said to me that I had a very normal childhood and have had a great life so far. "Writing that book isn't helping," she'd say. "It's only making you angrier!" I told her that my therapist, my wife and I thought it was very helpful for me to move forward from my anger in the hopes of having a normal happy life and not end up being like Dad.

Over time, it became obvious that I was writing a book about the role my parents (most specifically my dad) played during my childhood, intentionally or not, in corrupting my life by molding me to be just like them.

Everything I knew about America or the world growing up came from Dad and the extreme organizations he supported and peddled. Now that I'm forty-seven years-old, more open-minded and have access to the internet, I've been able to study history, facts, organizations, individuals, documents and events throughout modern history. As a result, I have come to an entirely new perspective on what has and is happening with America and even more specifically - angry Americans.

Grasping all the nonsense that Dad used to brainwash me when he had that power has allowed me to realize how monstrous his actions were and what Mom's role was in allowing him to raise her son in his image.

I certainly don't blame them for any of the mistakes or poor decisions I've made, and I've made a lot of them. I'll take full credit for all the stupid things I've done in this life. On the other hand, the reason I'm an overachiever in most everything I do is because I'm scared to death of becoming a complete loser like them.

Regardless of how I feel about my parents today, I was taught to believe that the John Birch Society was an educational organization that existed to keep America free. I was taught that if you loved America, you had to be a member and you had to educate other Americans about the Conspiracy. I was taught that conservatives of the extreme right-wing fringe were absolutely correct and they were the only entity in America who were truthful, moral and fighting to save America by educating our fellow Americans.

Sad to say, I wasn't just a prepubescent teen in the eighties assisting the extreme right-wing in their fight to save America with the truth. I was being prepped to kill and die for the cause when the time was right.

Robert Welch, in his *Blue Book*, stepped away from his education and rhetoric of "Less government, more responsibility, and - with God's help - a better world," (John Birch Society motto)[1] to a call to action. "This is a world-wide battle, the first in history, between light and darkness; between freedom and slavery; between the spirit of Christianity and the spirit of anti-Christ for the souls and bodies of men.... Let's win it even with our lives, if the time comes when we must." In a cult-like fashion, he adds these lines comparing the fight against commies to Jesus' fight to make men holy. "In the beauty of the lilies Christ was born across the sea, with a glory in His bosom that transfigures you and me: as He died to make men holy, let us die to make men free, while god is marching on."[2]

So when the Birchers say, "truth" is their only weapon in fighting the Communist Conspiracy, that's not true since they also preached militant efforts. Robert Welch clearly suggested in the *Blue Book* that I should "give up my life if the time comes when we must" to keep America free. For over sixty-five years now, the John Birch Society has been preaching that the horrors of communist enslavement are at our doorsteps.[3] How was I supposed to know when the time had come? Have all the murders in America committed by right-wing extremists happened because the time had come for the murderers?

To understand extremist violence, domestic terrorism and murder at the hands of a right-wing nut job in America today, one has to understand the source of inspiration.

The John Birch Society is the invisible culprit who has been encouraging deadly right-wing extremist violence in America since 1958. Even today, those who are aware of the John Birch Society think of it as a bunch of old conservative cranks who want to "Get us Out of the U.N." among other things. They're regarded as a political organization representing the right-wing extreme fringe of America. They're oftentimes not regarded as a militia-type organization although, clearly, their founder and dead leader had no problem with extreme political violence in America.

He encouraged it.

To say that the Timothy McVeigh's and every other right-wing maniac with a bomb or a gun wasn't inspired by Robert Welch and the John Birch Society is inaccurate. More likely than not, most acts of right-wing terrorism in America are inspired by the extremism in Welch's revolutionary *Blue Book* which ultimately laid the groundwork for fear, paranoia and right-wing extremist violence in America.

I'm not suggesting that the John Birch Society as an entity advocates to its membership that they should go blow up federal office buildings or assassinate left-wing celebrities or liberal politicians (although they certainly celebrate and enjoy their deaths).

Dad was thrilled when Pete Seeger, Nelson Mandela, Ted Kennedy, Rock Hudson, Liberace, Marvin Gaye, Ted Knight and Walter Cronkite all died. He considered their deaths something to celebrate.

What I'm stating is that with any extremist hate organization feeding hate propaganda constantly, it's inevitable that some followers or members are likely to feel the urge to pick up a machine gun or a rental truck loaded with a ton of ammonium nitrate and with "God's help if the time comes when we must," attempt to make this place a "better world." Of course, the John Birch Society has never taken credit for any deadly right-wing terrorist attacks in America.

When I first heard of Timothy McVeigh's horrible act of extreme right-wing domestic terrorism and the 168 people murdered (all Americans) in 1995, I wasn't surprised at all. In fact, I wasn't shocked or horrified. I was rather numb about the whole thing. I had a strong feeling it was the work of an extreme right-wing terrorist who blew up most of the Alfred P Murrah building in Oklahoma City before the news on television told us it was.

Frightening as it sounds now, bombing a federal office building had at one time made a lot of sense to me. McVeigh killed all those people to wake America up from the horrors and atrocities committed by the federal government against our own citizens - specifically to "correct the abuse of power" by federal agents against American citizens in the Ruby Ridge and Waco incidents. I used to think this way. Collateral damage is understood and acceptable when at war.

Unfortunately, the "time had come" for McVeigh and he knew that the ATF, FBI and perhaps the DEA had agents working in this building and so deemed it to be an appropriate target.[4] McVeigh also considered "a campaign of individual assassinations, with eligible targets to include: Federal Judge Walter Smith (Waco trial), Lon Horiuchi (FBI sniper at Ruby Ridge) and Janet Reno..." He wrote this in a note to Rita Cosby, senior correspondent for Fox News in April 2001.

Thomas Jefferson wrote, "The tree of liberty must be refreshed from time to time with the blood of patriots and tyrants."[5] Timothy McVeigh and I both knew this very popular and misunderstood quote well. The day that McVeigh killed all those people, he was wearing a t-shirt that had Jefferson's words on it with an image of a tree with blood dripping off the branches. What the extreme right-wing radicals didn't tell McVeigh was that in the same letter, Jefferson also wrote that the rebellion was "founded in ignorance ... The people cannot be all, and always, well-informed. The part which is wrong will be discontented in proportion to the importance of the facts they misconceive."

Misquoting our Founding Fathers isn't limited to domestic terrorists like McVeigh; it's also something that our elected officials do as well. A recent gun control measure in Washington State was found to be full of fake quotes from our Founding Fathers. "The measure, sponsored by state Rep. Matt Shea, R- Spokane Valley, would create penalties for public officials who block people from owning or buying guns. Almost an entire page of the four-page bill is dedicated to quotes from the Founding Fathers on gun ownership. But at least three of the quotes - attributed to Thomas Jefferson, George Washington and Alexander Hamilton - aren't real."[6]

These are just two tragic and sad examples of how pathetic and destructive the extreme right-wing is when it comes to quoting our Founding Fathers to justify their own radical actions. Dad always quoted the Founding Fathers to me when I was young. I never knew or questioned whether the words were true or not.

In looking back at the Oklahoma City Bombing, it shocks me to realize that McVeigh and I weren't so different growing up. We were both avid readers of *Soldier of Fortune* magazine and we both frequented gun shows. We were both into survivalist techniques - stockpiling survival equipment and weapons (in case the commies took over). We both loved movies such as "Red Dawn" and the "Rambo" series and dreamed about those scenarios becoming our reality.

We grew up in predominantly white communities. McVeigh had written a letter to his local newspaper complaining about taxation much like my letter to the local newspaper complaining that they were misrepresenting the type of government we have.

McVeigh saw himself as a hero - an American patriot and a

righteous Christian soldier who was becoming a prisoner fighting a war against America's most evil enemy - the American government. This was the exact same sentiment I had when I was young. I was an American patriot and I wanted to be a hero. I wanted to make my Dad proud.

McVeigh was six months older than me, but his mind had been lost permanently to the fringes of the extreme right. His anger and paranoia were fueled by a few of his chosen adult peers. Sadly, McVeigh lost his mental balance after reading *The Turner Diaries*, an insane novel by William Pierce who was also a member of the John Birch Society and the leader of the American Nazi movement. We had a copy of *The Turner Diaries* in our house when I was living there.

McVeigh didn't experience brainwashing about the evils of the Communist Conspiracy growing up like I did. McVeigh's parents didn't push or encourage him to read this book or others. He did this on his own as a young adult. He made a choice and his parents were horrified about what he did. My dad thinks McVeigh is an American hero. He told me so.

Had Ruby Ridge happened in the mid-eighties instead of the early nineties, I'm not sure that I'd be alive today. During that time, I was dedicated to the ideals of the John Birch Society, to fighting the Communist Conspiracy and "killing 'em all" if "the time" ever came. I'm certain the horrors of what happened at Ruby Ridge would have had the same effect on me as it did McVeigh - if not more so.

I paid little attention to the events that happened in Ruby Ridge in 1992. I didn't obsess about it and all I knew was what I saw on the mainstream news. Even when Dad was sending me copies of *The New American* after I moved out, I hardly ever looked at them.

According to the *New York Times*, well over half of all terrorism attacks in America are committed by "white supremacists, anti-government fanatics and other non-Muslim extremists."[7]

As of 2011, there were over 1,000 official hate groups in the United States.[8]

The election and re-election of a black man as President of the United States has spurred the increase in the number of these groups. The vast majority of them have beliefs and agendas inspired by the John Birch Society.

The truly stunning growth came in the anti-government 'patriot' movement - conspiracy-minded groups that see the federal government as their primary enemy."[9] This rhetoric is John Birch Society 101 and dates back to 1958 when the hate group was created.

There were an official 148 "patriot" groups in America during George Bush's last year as president in 2008. That number rose to 512 during Obama's first year and then skyrocketed to 1360 patriot groups when he was reelected for a second term in 2012.[10]

Most if not all home-grown domestic terrorists proclaim themselves to be patriotic Americans and God-fearing Christians who love Jesus. They are more than willing to kill government employees, politicians, celebrities, school kids, Black people, Jews or anyone who gets in the way simply to "wake us all up" to the supposed horrors committed by our federal government. The "time has come" for many of them.

Like McVeigh, they justify their actions by pointing to the Waco and Ruby Ridge incidents. They believe that if they don't strike soon, it will all be too late. They believe that it's their patriotic duty to kill anyone who stands in the way of their version of America. I know this kind of thinking to be true. I used to believe the same thing.

When the father of Dylan Klebold's (one of the two perpetrators of the Columbine High School massacre in which twelve students and one teacher were murdered in 1999) found out what his son had done on the day of the massacre, he said in disbelief, "That was not my son."

In *The New American* article titled, "Columbine Revisited: What Have We Learned?," the John Birch Society blamed the public education system for the murders and said that Columbine High School's "hatred of God" was to blame.

The article further goes on about how "few parents understand the gap that atheist schooling (public schools) can create between them and their children."[11] According to the John Birch Society, all Americans who went to a public school received atheist training that has enabled them to kill American children.

The other perpetrator in the Columbine Killings, Eric Harris, had a journal that contained entries from both kids about events such as the Oklahoma City Bombing, the Waco Siege, the Vietnam War and how they wished to "outdo" these events. It was mostly about what McVeigh had done four years earlier including how both killers got the guns they used from a local gun show.[12]

The Columbine killers killed because of hate rhetoric and conspiracy theories from the extreme right, not because they received atheist training from America's public school system.

Every time there's an act of domestic terrorism or a mass shooting or a bombing in America, Dad always proclaims that it wasn't real or if it was real, the federal government staged the event in an attempt to take away our guns and freedoms.

Dad among many others doesn't believe that the Newtown School Massacre actually happened. He thinks Obama planned the Aurora Theatre Killings in Colorado to implement radical gun control legislation. He believes McVeigh was set up. Dad believes 911 was an inside job. Every time there's a mass murder in America involving a right-wing extremist, Dad says it's not real, and is going to be used as a reason for the government to take away our guns.

Like Dad, one of the two brothers suspected of the Boston Bombings in 2013 possessed literature stating that both 9/11 and the Oklahoma Bombing were government conspiracies.[13]

The ridiculous comparison that the extreme right draws on is by using the similarities between the German disarmament laws and modern gun control legislation in America. Clearly there are huge differences between limiting the availability of fully-automatic machine guns to civilians versus a complete elimination of firearms. Such comparisons by folks like Dad defy logical reasoning and have no basis in reality. My dad believes, along with Ted Cruz, Donald Trump, Ted Nugent, Sarah Palin, McVeigh and others, that any piece of gun legislation is a huge step toward the future Communist States of America.

This paranoia isn't limited to just the crazed right-winger hiding their assault rifle under the sheets or the open-carry nut jobs walking around in plain daylight with an AR-15 strapped to their back, (exercising their "God-given" constitutional rights) either. Texas Republican Rep. Steve Stockman said "any proposal to abuse executive power and infringe upon gun rights must be repelled with the stiffest legislative force possible." This was his response after President Obama floated the possibility of using executive action to enact policies aimed at reducing gun violence following the Sandy Hook Elementary School shooting. The one-term congressman concluded that the executive order would be "not just an attack on the Constitution, but also an attack on Americans."[14]

James Yeager, CEO of Tactical Response, a gun and tactical training outfit, responded to Obama's failed gun control efforts in 2013 by stating that any gun control actions on behalf of the Obama Administration would "spark a civil war" and that he would be "glad to fire the first shot." He added, "And I need all you patriots to start thinking about what you're going to do, load your damn mags, make sure your rifle's clean, pack a backpack with some food in it and get ready to fight." Tactical Response had over 40,000 likes on Facebook in February 2016.[15]

The heavily right-winged NRA responded to the Sandy Hook massacre by suggesting a program to put armed security guards in all schools across the country increasing the number of "armed" people in America.[16]

Obama never did implement any legislation to try to prevent more mass murders in America after the Sandy Hook mass murders.

Dad says that gun control would never work because criminals won't give them up and there will still be crime. Dad says that only "good law abiding white Americans would obey gun control laws and then all us white people would be vulnerable to crime and tyranny." He failed to mention that he and all of his buddies on the extreme right would never under any circumstance give up their millions of unregistered guns either.

Dad also said that gun control was ridiculous because even if the government did take away our guns, people who wanted to kill other people could still do so with butter knives. Then he'd suggest to me that it would be only a matter of time before the government enacted a ban on butter knives. This was the kind of logic I knew when I was young.

The United States has some of the laxest gun control laws on the planet today. There are almost as many legally-owned guns (if not more) in America as there are Americans.[17] This is the highest ratio for any country on the planet. This also doesn't take into the account the number of illegally-owned guns which the government can't track. Not one firearm in Dad's arsenal is registered.

Frankly, I'm surprised there aren't more attacks on federal and state government buildings or public schools, college campuses, day care centers, movie theaters, hospitals, shopping malls and other places. I'm never surprised when there's a mass-killing in America. I'm horrified, saddened, but never shocked. I was conditioned for this violence and ready for these attacks and killings after Larry McDonald died in 1983.

It doesn't surprise me when a bunch of militia members engage in a stand-off with federal agents in the desert or take over a wildlife refuge in the middle of nowhere. In my mind, there's been an unofficial war going on between the so-called patriots in America and the American government my entire life. Nothing that an extreme right-wing nut job does or says surprises me.

The conspiracies and paranoia that right-wing extremists subscribe to are the same that I was brainwashed to believe as a child. The extremism, racism and paranoia that has been or is being spoken by Ammon and Cliven Bundy, Donald Trump, Ted and Rafael Cruz, Alex Jones, Glenn Beck and many other public figures is the same that Dad preached to me growing up.

"It's not difficult to diagnose the Oregon militia as having been heavily brainwashed by the eliminationism rhetoric... with its "Don't retreat, reload" bumper sticker slogans, backed up by the revolutionary predictions of conspiracy-theory profiteers like Glenn Beck and Alex Jones." Salon.com.[18]

Prior to the 2012 presidential election, right-wing extremists were still in the closet. That presidential election revealed a lot about America when extremism began making the gradual shift to mainstream and their cause gained a serious amount of traction. The extreme right was still kooky and a minority-fringe of the Republican Party when a black man became president.

Four years later, when Obama sought reelection, extremists such as the Tea Party were up in arms and ready to revolt. In many instances, they did.

The strength that the Ron Paul movement gained along with the support he received from the KKK, the John Birch Society, the Tea Party and others signaled that our country was very much in trouble and a new civil war was brewing.

Ron Paul had done quite well for a while during the primaries of the 2012 presidential election. The extreme right, through shear vote count, realized that their base had dramatically grown. People were told that they should be angry and they were getting screwed by the government and many, many people believed in this message. Neither Barry Goldwater nor George Wallace were able to achieve this high level of paranoia with this type of message as the presidential candidates have in 2016.

The extreme on the far right are no longer the fringe movement that William J. Buckley described and warned us about in 1962.[19] The extreme right-wing has visibly overthrown the Republican Party where moderates like Senators John McCain and John Boehner are called traitors by the extremists. "There is a truly treasonous form of evil afloat in the Republican controlled House of Representatives and his name is John Boehner," says christianpoliticalparty.com.[20] "With McCain (Sen. John) supporters continually touting his heroism and attacking Democrats that served honorably in Vietnam like John Kerry and Al Gore, the unavoidable embarrassment is that their standard bearer may have been the biggest American traitor since Benedict Arnold," says veteranstoday.com.[21]

Dad would often say that moderates in the Republican Party were traitors and actually worse than the commies. Even in March 2016 as the presidential election draws near, Republican presidential candidates like Donald Trump, Ben Carson and Ted Cruz reveal that the ideology and paranoia of the extreme right is heavily seeded within the front-runners. There is little question that the Republican Party will most likely nominate a right-wing extremist to be their candidate of choice.

Watching these candidates and previous ones on the televised debates with my wife and son is very entertaining, embarrassing and frightening at the same time. Most of these candidates echo things that my Dad has been saying for decades. For the most part, they sound like they are all members complaining about anything and everything at a local John Birch Society Chapter meeting.

Constantly hearing presidential candidates spew nonsense and lies on a daily basis is overwhelming. The things I hear today on cable news are in many situations no different than the rhetoric I heard when I was a young impressionable preteen.

So runs the Birch fantasy, spun out in dozens of books distributed in millions of copies and videos, websites and cable news shows. Millions of Americans now believe in a conspiracy that America is under attack from Muslims, ISIS, gays, blacks, illegal Mexican immigrants, Chinese, Russians, Iranians, women, Jews, environmentalists, liberals, hippies, Clinton, Obama, Sanders, Satan and more.

"These Americans thrive on hate and conspiracy theories, many fed to them by politicians and commentators who blithely blather about government concentration camps, impending martial law and plans to seize guns along with other dystopian gibberish, apparently unaware there are people listening who don't know it's all lies. These extremists turn to violence - against minorities, non- Christians, abortion providers, and government officials - in what they believe is a fight to save America. And that the potential for violence is escalating every day." *Newsweek.*[22]

The top three Republican candidates (Trump, Cruz and Rubio) for president (as of March 2016) are self-declared patriots who are contemptuous of the entire Democratic Party and, most elected officials in Washington DC in either party. They breathe anger. They're divisive, radical and ridiculous. They behave as schoolyard bullies and not only seem to attack everything and anything, but they also attack each other.

Though not likely official because their membership lists are secret, the non-fringe John Birch Society of 2016 has clearly won the 2016 Republican Presidential primary. These top Republican presidential candidates are role models for what the Birch Society has been envisioning for American for over half a century now. For the first time ever, the John Birch Society, KKK and the Tea Party will have a mainstream major party candidate who more resembles their goals, desires and ideals than ever before.

Even if the Republican nominee fails at the general election, the John Birch Society, the Tea Party and every other hate organization that once stood fast on the fringe of right-wing politics, will be stronger, larger, richer and further along their path to creating the America that they envision.

If one of the Democratic nominees wins, these extremist groups will have a declared Democratic socialist or a woman to hate and attack for at least the next four years. This hate, anger and paranoia that fuel the extreme right-wing isn't going to go away anytime soon.

The late Senator Joseph McCarthy whose notable anti-communist crusades damaged the lives and reputations of thousands of Americans with only flimsy information provided as if it was factual and without any sense of decency, would most certainly feel welcome in today's

Republican Party - more so than ever before.

Of course Birch Society founder Robert Welch, who spent most of his adult life identifying himself as a Republican, was often very critical of moderates and mainstream ideas within the party itself. Without question, Welch too would be thrilled and likely declare that victory is near with the current state of the 2016 Republican Party (assuming that Trump wins the general election).

The incredible growth of right-wing extremism in America is horrifying. The shift towards total extremism now features echoes of an unconstitutional dictatorship, fascist state or monarchy. These candidates are constantly speaking words that are un-American, unchristian-like, offensive, racist, sexist, unconstitutional, and they're bringing in a record numbers of voters supporting them.

Watching Trump yell and mock protestors at his rallies is unfortunate and shocking. In a growing number of incidents, violence is occurring.[23]

He spends a lot of time and energy blaming certain minorities for our country's problems. On March 5th, 2016, he went as far as asking the crowd at his rally to raise their right hands and swear that they would vote for him and said that "bad things happen if you don't live up to what you just did."[24]

In February 2016, Ben Carson taking a page right out of the John Birch Society, said during a Republican Presidential debate, "Joseph Stalin said if you want to bring America down you have to undermine three things - our spiritual life, our patriotism, and our morality."[25] Not many questioned what he said as it pretty much went along with the theme of most Republican debates and sounded as if the quote was ripped out of a John Birch Society or Tea Party pamphlet warning us of the evils of communism. The audience applauded Carson and the other candidates nodded with approval. Problem was, however, the quote wasn't real or even close to real. Carson likely saw it as a meme on Facebook and repeated the lie in front of a nationally televised audience.

Consider what Representative Allen West (R-Fla) said in 2012 while he was under serious consideration to be the GOP's vice-presidential nominee, "I believe there are about 78 to 81 members of the Democratic Party that are members of the Communist Party."[26] It was too soon for the Republican Party in 2012 to have such an extremist on board for the position of vice president so he was ruled out. If West had said such nonsense in early 2016, he'd fit right in.

Pastor Rafael Cruz, father of Senator Ted Cruz said, "Barrack Obama said: If the winds shift, I will side with the Muslims" at a Republican Party dinner in September 2013.[27] This is a complete lie and his followers were enraged. Like Carson, Rafael didn't make up that quote. He read it elsewhere, found it interesting and started repeating it as the truth. President Obama never said such a thing. But, when listeners of the father of Ted Cruz hear this, they become outraged and start repeating the lie - all the time thinking that they're speaking the truth.

The fruit doesn't fall very from the tree in the case of Ted Cruz, who very likely will go down as one of the biggest liars in modern history. "Cruz's *Politifact* track record for publicly-asserted falsehoods is the second-highest among front-runners, totaling 56 percent of all statements they've looked at," according to the *Daily Beast*. Ben Carson wins with telling more fibs than any other candidate.[28]

One ultimate problem with all of these politicians and people like my dad, however, is oftentimes when they are telling a lie they don't know that they're telling a lie. And, because they completely trust the source of their information (even if it is a meme on Facebook), they don't question it. Like Cruz, my dad is a liar who perpetuates his misinformation to anyone who will listen. If he is presented with the truth and facts that destroy what he knows, he'll reject it. Matter of fact, Dad will adamantly fight against any sets of facts, science or evidence that would persuade him to give up his falsehoods. Further, a confrontation will cause him to support his set of lies even more strongly.

I seriously wonder what the impacts of the hateful words echoed by some of these presidential candidates, whether they get elected or not, will mean for the future of America and most importantly, for my son.

How many other children are watching these debates with their parents who applaud when a candidate says we should kill all family members of terrorists or that we're being screwed over by the Japanese, Chinese, Mexicans, Iranians, Russians and others and we should hate them? Are these kids going to grow up repeating the cycle of hate?

This country survived the assassination of Martin Luther King Jr. It survived the McCarthy witch hunts and the violent racism from George Wallace. We survived 9/11 and I'm hopeful we'll survive the 2016 Presidential elections. For now, though, I can only hope that America will elect a president who isn't full of anger and hate.

Ultimately, it's a complete lack of self-respect, self-awareness and low self-esteem that inspires right-wing extremists to be so angry. They criticize and attack anyone who isn't in agreement with their views. Most of these people presumably hate themselves and the lives they live. Rather than deal with their own anger, they combine it with hatred to feel better about themselves and what they stand for.

EPILOGUE

LOVE OR BE LOVED

The greatest fear I have is the fear that I'm being just like my father or will end up being just like him. While this fear no longer keeps me up at night, it's a real and valid fear that I will always have.

Hating myself is something that I refuse to do now. When you hate yourself, it takes no effort to hate someone else rather than showing them love. When you hate yourself, it's impossible to love someone else.

It's taken me over three decades to finally overcome my anger and hate. I was in complete denial for the longest time when I was an angry person.

I would often get asked, "Why are you so angry?" Or, "Why are you mad?" I would always deny that I was mad or in a bad mood and mock the other person (mostly my wife) for being ridiculous.

Only in the past few years have I been able to admit that I've been an angry person and have been for a long time. I always had to be mad. I always had to hate someone or something and I've always had to have an enemy.

I couldn't be happy, content or grateful. These were the examples Dad demonstrated to me and what he brainwashed me into believing when I was young. I was entitled, greedy and selfish and had been immersed in this destructive behavior for well over thirty years, not knowing why I was so angry.

Looking back, I was angry because my behavior patterns were like Dad's. I knew that in order for me to be happy and successful, I'd have to be nothing like him. Yet, it was always a struggle to not revert into being a critical prick like him. Be it low self-esteem or being completely unaware of who I am, paranoia always played a role in my well-being. The results of such destructive thought-patterns led me to deceive myself and caused me to often sabotage my true happiness.

I can clearly see the effects of not having a normal childhood in which trust, honesty and my best interests were never put first. Mine was unorganized, full of inconsistent realities and completely lacking in honesty and kindness.

Only now have I shut down the filth, paranoia and lunacy from both of my parents. I've shut them out mentally, emotionally, intellectually and now physically. This has finally allowed me to move forward as a real person. I've truly found peace and happiness.

I think the reason why I've never killed anyone or blown anything up is, ultimately, because I really loved my parents and wanted them to love me back. My therapist assures me that this is true. If I were the kind of person who didn't seek love or approval from my parents, I may very well have committed some horrible atrocities. I've always wanted to make my parents proud and I've spent most of life trying to do so.

No matter what I do or what I've done, not being like Dad makes me a failure in his eyes. He hates me because I'm not like him. I don't know if it's because his cloning tactics and brainwashing failed or if it's because he truly knows that I'm a much better, smarter and happier person than he could ever be. Maybe he's jealous and that's why he hates me? Maybe he knows that what he believes is wrong and cruel and he can't make himself stop because he's too far immersed in it?

Regardless of how much I tried to make Dad proud of me, I knew he was wrong about most of what he taught me. My dad is and always has been an ignorant fool. I've never let him know I believe this. Some people have told him how wrong and ridiculous he has been. He's written those people off. "Brainwashed or brain dead," he'd say about anyone who didn't agree with him. I've never told him how wrong and idiotic he is, but I'm sure he knows what I think and that's why he's finally written me off.

There is something seriously and deadly wrong in America when racists, sexists, paranoids and those full of hatred brainwash their children with their own narrow-minded belief systems and hypocritical moral compass. To bring a child into this world - only for the purpose of creating a "mini me," rather than a unique, individual person - is selfish, cruel and unforgivable. As long as ignorant extremists breed and do their best at cloning themselves, racism, hate and bigotry in America will continue to thrive. This will continue and get worse over generations unless more and more adult children stand up to their parents and reject their mindless and soulless paranoia.

When I see and hear politicians and right-wing domestic terrorists in their forties and fifties speaking the same hatred that came out of my father's mouth - I get a bad feeling in the pit of my stomach knowing that they too were most likely brainwashed by their fathers and have spent their lives trying make their fathers proud as well. There's no question that Ted Cruz, as a perfect example, is loved and adored by his father. He is ideologically like his father. He walks in his dad's footsteps and repeats the same paranoia, hatred and nonsense.

This is a repeating pattern of ignorance that humans display in order to attain love and affection from their parents and it's just plain sad. It ticks me off that Ted Cruz is loved and respected by his father.

He's a puppet, a clone, a duplicate of his lying, angry and paranoid father. For this, Ted is loved and adored. His father is proud of him for being just like him while I'm hated by my dad for being myself.

As much as I despise Ted, I feel a great sense of success in knowing that unlike him and many others, I was able to break free from my dad's paranoia, hatred and ignorance. I've been able to become my own person with my own thoughts and ideals - not just a pathetic and weak-minded puppet of my dad.

My son is now seventeen and one of the smartest, most selfless and self-aware humans that I've ever known. He is smart, aware and open-minded. He is handsome, kind and bright. He's a happy kid with a great future in front of him.

My wife has been an active voice of reason and compassion throughout the process of raising our son. She would not sit back and watch me attempt to corrupt him. She was active and involved.

She's been a great mother and a truly understanding wife. She believed the most important quality that we could instill in him would be empathy. She's a genius.

Our son knows that he can believe whatever he wants and vote for whomever he wants when he's old enough. He is a person - his own person. He's not me. We may disagree on things, have discussions but no matter what, we love each other and respect each other's opinions. He is an intelligent individual and not a racist, sexist, bigot or angry jerk.

I love my son. There's nothing that will ever change this. My son loves me and that will never change. We even like each other! He means the world to me. I love him so much that words can't describe how I feel. No matter what, he will be loved.

END NOTES

Chapter 2: The John Birch Society

1. https://archive.org/stream/TheBlueBook/MicrosoftWordDocument1_dj vu.txt
2. http://www.newyorker.com/magazine/2010/10/18/confoundingfathers
3. http://www.academia.edu/7263327/The_Increasing_Popularity_of_Rig ht_Wing_Conspiracy_Theories
4. http://www.jbs.org/issues-pages/united-nations
5. http://www.jbs.org/issues-pages/united-nations
6. http://cnsnews.com/news/article/barbara-hollingsworth/cruz-vowsrip-obamas-iranian-nuke-deal-shreds
7. http://www.dallasnews.com/news/jfk50/reflect/20131012extremists-in-dallas-created-volatile-atmosphere-before-jfks-1963visit.ece
8. http://www.theworld-aroundus.com/people/10-people-who-shaped-the-illuminati-conspiracy-theory/4/
9. https://birchwatcher.files.wordpress.com/2015/03/whats_wrong_with_c ivil_rights.png
10. http://publicdomainreview.org/2014/04/02/darkness-over-all-john-robison-and-the-birth-of-the-illuminati-conspiracy/
11. http://www.eveningsun.com/story/news/local/blogs/inside-the-sun/2012/06/09/does-fluoride-affect-critical-thinking-skills/32083633/
12. http://www.msnbc.com/transcripts/rachel-maddow-show/2009-12-23
13. http://mormonheretic.org/2010/11/15/benson-eisenhower-andcommunism/

14. http://www.jbs.org/about-jbs/john-birch
15. https://www.youtube.com/watch?v=nLWXpubTjE&lc=1yZzRDtF6ilY
    4gHONM6jHWmxx8PVfyiJfoGZFX-dmv0
16. http://articles.latimes.com/1985-01-08/news/mn-7296_1_john-
    birchsociety
17. http://www.robertwelchuniversity.org/Politician-Final2.pdf
18. http://thinkprogress.org/politics/2011/06/10/242334/john-birchsociety-
    celebrates-koch/
19. https://www.newspapers.com/newspage/1390851/
20. https://en.wikipedia.org/wiki/Gertz_v._Robert_Welch,_Inc.
21. http://www.newyorker.com/magazine/2016/01/11/a-view-from-the-
    fringe
22. https://tpzoo.wordpress.com/2010/01/01/rachel-maddow-talks-about-
    the-john-birch-society/
23. http://www.ellensplace.net/ar_pboy.html

Chapter 4: An Ignorant Man is Half as Dangerous as an Educated Fool

1. http://aphelis.net/cult-ignorance-isaac-asimov-1980/

Chapter 5: Summertime Blues

2. http://www.jbs.org/campus-liberty-alliance/who-moved-my-camp-
   february-2009
3. Robert Welch, *JBS Bulletin*, February 1973
4. Raven Clabough, *The New American*, August 12, 2011

Chapter 6: None Dare Call it a Conspiracy

1. https://en.wikipedia.org/wiki/Larry_McDonald
2. http://www.jbs.org/rep-larry-mcdonald
3. https://www.youtube.com/watch?v=94MUDQc1L9cHelen Dewar and
   Vivian Aplin-Brownlee, "Rep. McDonald Hailed As Right-Wing
   Martyr," *The Washington Post*, 9/2/1983
4. https://www.youtube.com/watch?v=puNCkwjuxJ0
5. "Widow Blames Russians," *Bangor Daily News*, 9/2/1983
6. Section 4, Page 7, full page advertisement, *Chicago Tribune*,
   11/15/1983
7. Robert W. Lee, "KAL 007 Remembered, The Questions Remain

Unanswered," *The New American*, September 1991.

8. http://www.rescue007.org/helms_letter.htm

9. Walter E Williams, "Liberal and Progressive Vision," *The New American*, October 2015

10. Norman D Sandler, "President Reagan demanded reparations from the Soviet Union Monday... ," UPI Archives, 9/5/1983.

11. *The Blue Book*, Robert Welch, 1958.

Chapter 7: A Dead Liberal is a Good Liberal

1. http://www.thedemocraticstrategist.org/strategist/2011/01/the_slippery_slope_of_violent.php

Chapter 8: It's the End of the World and I Know it

1. http://www.costco.com/8,600-Total-Servings-1-Person-1-yearFood-Storage.product.100003177.html

2. http://www.walmart.com/ip/Augason-Farms-Deluxe-1-Year-1-Person-Emergency-Food-Storage-Kit-120-count/22001495

3. https://en.wikipedia.org/wiki/Doomsday_Preppers

4. http://pjmedia.com/lifestyle/2012/11/29/doomsday-preppers-week3-child-abuse/

5. Caroline Bankoff, *New York Magazine*, "Newtown Shooter Adam Lanza's Mother was an Avid Gun Collector, December 16, 2012

6. http://www.biography.com/people/adam-lanza-21068899

7. http://www.washingtonpost.com/wpsrv/national/longterm/oklahoma/bg/mcveigh.htm

8. http://www.history.com/this-day-in-history/olympic-park-bomber-eric-rudolph-agrees-to-plead-guilty

9. http://www.seattletimes.com/seattle-news/north-bend-murdersuspect-found-dead-in-bunker/

10. http://www.history.com/this-day-in-history/federal-agents-raidthe-branch-davidian-compound-in-waco-texas

11. http://www.spokesman.com/stories/2012/aug/19/ruby-ridgecarved-niche-history/

12. http://www.cnn.com/2005/ALLPOLITICS/01/20/bush.speech/

13. http://breakingdefense.com/2013/05/no-longer-unthinkableshould- us-ready-for-limited-nuclear-war/

14. http://www.cnn.com/2015/07/09/politics/joseph-dunford-russia-greatest-threat/
15. http://coursesa.matrix.msu.edu/~hst306/documents/indust.html
16. http://history.jburroughs.org/cfront/us45/readings/ike_forpol2.htm
17. http://spartacus-educational.com/JFKwelchR.htm
18. http://theweek.com/articles/580740/ben-carson-ready-coming-american-apocalypse
19. https://www.youtube.com/watch?v=e_Rn1K5uLzs
20. http://www.salon.com/2009/09/16/beck_skousen/
21. http://www.newsweek.com/2014/05/02/militiamen-fight-overcliven-bundys-ranch-far-over-248354.html

Chapter 10: The Effects of Teaching Your Child to be a Paranoid

1. "John Birch Society Still Rolls On," Philip Noble, *Universal Press*, November 13, 1976
2. "Off-Duty Soldiers Shoot It Out With Drug Suspects," UPI, *LA Times*, September 25, 1989

Chapter 11: Brave Man's Death

1. http://www.history.army.mil/books/dahsum/1990-91/ch07.htm
2. http://www.presidency.ucsb.edu/ws/?pid=18820
3. http://www.nytimes.com/2002/08/18/world/officers-say-us-aided-iraq-in-war-despite-use-of-gas.html
4. http://www.thenewamerican.com/culture/history/item/20780-whatif-anything-have-we-learned-from-the-vietnam-war

Chapter 16: Old Man

1. http://www.sfgate.com/entertainment/morford/article/The-Sad-Quotable-Jerry-Falwell-It-s-bad-form-3302297.php
2. "In Defense of American liberties: A History of the ACLU," by Samuel Walker, Page 252.
3. The Empire Strikes Back, George Lucas

Chapter 17: Where it's at

1 http://www.jbs.org/about-jbs/history
2 https://archive.org/stream/*TheBlueBook*/MicrosoftWordDocument1_dj

vu.txt

3   https://archive.org/stream/*TheBlueBook*/MicrosoftWordDocument1_dj vu.txt

4   https://en.wikipedia.org/wiki/Timothy_McVeigh

5   https://www.loc.gov/exhibits/jefferson/105.html

6   http://www.theolympian.com/news/politicsgovernment/article58711873.html

7   http://www.nytimes.com/2015/06/25/us/tally-of-attacks-in-uschallenges- perceptions-of-top-terror-threat.html?_r=0

8   https://www.splcenter.org/news/2011/02/23/us-hate-groups-top1000

9   https://www.splcenter.org/fighting-hate/intelligencereport/2012/patriot- movement-explodes

10 https://www.splcenter.org/fighting-hate/intelligencereport/2016/year-hate- and-extremism

11 http://www.thenewamerican.com/reviews/opinion/item/11150columbine- revisited-what-have-we-learned?

12 https://en.wikipedia.org/wiki/Eric_Harris_and_Dylan_Klebold

13 http://www.bbc.com/news/world-us-canada-23541341

14 http://www.politico.com/blogs/on-congress/2013/01/repstockman-threatens- obama-impeachment-over-guns-154141

15 http://www.rawstory.com/2013/01/unhinged-tactical-responseceo-threatens- to-start-killing-people-over-obamas-gun-control/

16 https://www.washingtonpost.com/politics/remarks-from-the-nrapress-conference-on-sandy-hook-school-shooting-delivered-on-dec21-2012-transcript/2012/12/21/bd1841fe4b8811e2a6a6aabac85e8036_story.html

17 http://www.motherjones.com/politics/2015/06/gun-owners-studyone-in-three

18 http://www.salon.com/2016/02/12/the_brainwashed_rebels_of_the_bundy_siege_why_something_like_this_was_eventually_bound_to_happen

19 https://en.wikipedia.org/wiki/William_F._Buckley,_Jr

20 http://christianpoliticalparty.com/john-boehner-is-a-traitor/

21 http://www.veteranstoday.com/2015/07/18/trump-right-abouthanoi-john- mccain/

22 http://www.newsweek.com/2016/02/12/right-wing-

extremistsmilitants- bigger-threat-america-isis-jihadists-422743.html

23 http://www.cnn.com/2016/02/23/politics/donald-trump-nevadarally-punch/

24 http://news.usa.extra.hu/latest/donald-trump-asks-supporters-toraise-right- hand-in-a-scene-straight-out-of-nazi-germany

25 http://www.politifact.com/truth-o-meter/statements/2016/feb/14/ben-carson/ ben-carson-flubs-stalinquote-about-bringing-down-/

26 https://www.washingtonpost.com/blogs/the-fix/post/republicanrep-allen-west-suggests-many-congressional-democrats-arecommunists/2012/04/11/ gIQApbZiAT_blog.html

27 http://www.rightwingwatch.org/content/ted-cruzs-dad-citesmanipulated-obama-quote-bogus-health-care-claim-incendiaryspeech

28 http://www.thedailybeast.com/articles/2015/03/22/the-truthbehind-ted-cruz-s-lies.htm